Compound 1080 Special Review Position Document 4

U.S. Environmental Protection Agency

United States
Environmental Protection
Agency

Office of
Pesticides and Toxic Substances
Washington, DC 20460

July 1985

Pesticides

&EPA

Compound 1080
Special Review Position
Document 4

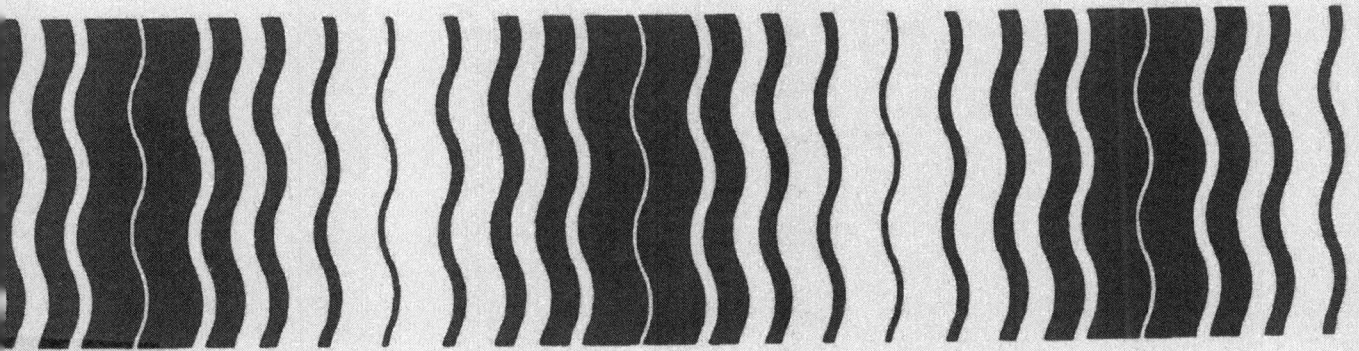

COMPOUND 1080

POSITION DOCUMENT 4

U. S. ENVIRONMENTAL PROTECTION AGENCY

OFFICE OF PESTICIDES AND TOXIC SUBSTANCES

OFFICE OF PESTICIDE PROGRAMS

401 M STREET, SW

WASHINGTON, D.C.   20460

July 1985

TABLE OF CONTENTS

Page

Executive Summary   i

I.   Introduction   1

     A. Background   1
     B. Position Document 1   2
     C. Summary of Actions Proposed in PD 2/3   3
     D. Organization of Position Document 4   5

II. Comments and Agency Response on the PD 2/3   6
     Risk Assessment

     A. General Comments on Risk Assessment   6

        1. Scientific Advisory Panel   6
        2. Wyoming Department of Agriculture   7
        3. Montana Department of Agriculture   8

     B. Lack of Emergency Treatment   9

        1. Agency Position in PD 2/3   9
        2. Comments on PD 2/3   9
        3. Agency Response   9

     C. Acute Toxicity to Mammals and Birds   10

        1. Agency Position in PD 2/3   10
        2. Comments on PD 2/3   11
        3. Agency Response   11

     D. Significant Adverse Effects on Populations of   12
        Nontarget Organisms

        1. Agency Position in PD 2/3   12

           a. General
           b. Direct Risks to Nontarget Species
           c. Indirect Risks to Nontarget Species
           d. Community Level Impacts
           e. Relation of Bait Formulations to Risks

        2. Comments on PD 2/3   17

           a. The Hegdal Study (1979)
           b. Predator/Prey Relationship
           c. Relationship of Bait Formulations to Risk
           d. Other Comments

         3. Agency Response   21

             a. The Hegdal Study
             b. Predator/Prey Relationship
             c. Relationship of Bait Formulations
                to Risk
             d. Other Comments

       E. Endangered Species   24

         1. California Condor   25

             a. Agency Position in PD 2/3
             b. Comments
             c. Agency Response
                                           29

         2. San Joaquin Kit Fox

             a. Agency Position in PD 2/3
             b. Comments
             c. Agency Response

         3. Black-footed ferret   33

             a. Agency Position in PD 2/3
             b. Comments
             c. Agency Response

         4. Aleutian Canada Goose   34

             a. Agency Position in PD 2/3
             b. Comments
             c. Agency Response

III. Comments and Agency Response on PD 2/3   36
     Benefits Analysis

   A. Agency Position in PD 2/3   36
   B. Comments on PD 2/3   37
   C. Agency Response   38
   D. New Information   40

IV. Comments and Agency Response on Proposed   41
     Regulatory Actions in Position Document

   A. Rangeland, Cropland, and Non-agricultural   41
      Sites: Ground Squirrels

     1. Proposed Actions in PD 2/3   41
     2. Comments on PD 2/3   42
     3. Agency Response   44

B. Rangeland and Cropland: Prairie Dogs   47

   1. Proposed Actions in PD 2/3   47
   2. Comments on PD 2/3   47
   3. Agency Response   49

C. Rangeland, Cropland, and Non-agricultural   50
   Sites Except Around Ships and Buildings:
   Other Rodents

   1. Proposed Actions in PD 2/3   50
   2. Comments on PD 2/3   51
   3. Agency Response   52

D. Use In and Around Ships and Buildings: 52
   Norway Rat, Roof Rat, and House Mice

E. General Comments on Proposed Actions   52

V.   Final Regulatory Decision   54

A. General   54

B. Rangeland, Cropland, and Non-agricultural   56
   Sites: Ground Squirrels

   1. Reduction and Standardization of Bait   56
      Concentration and Application Rates
   2. Standardization of Hand Baiting and   57
      Post-Baiting Procedures
   3. Standardization of Aerial Baiting and   57
      Post-Baiting Procedures
   4. Special Restrictions for Endangered   58
      Species Protection
   5. Other Label Statements   58

C. Rangeland and Cropland: Prairie Dogs   58

D. Rangeland, Cropland, and Non-agricultural   59
   Sites Except Around Ships and Buildings:
   Other Rodents

E. Use In and Around Ships and Buildings: 60
   Norway Rat, Roof Rat, and House Mice

F. Summary of Regulatory Requirements   60

   1. General Requirements   60

     a. Hand Baiting and Post-Baiting Procedures   60
     b. Nontarget Species Label Precaution   61
     c. Restricted Use Classification Label   61
       Statement
     d. Bait Dyes   62

2. Rangeland, Cropland and   62
   Non-agricultural Sites: Ground Squirrels

   a. Bait Concentration Levels   62
   b. Aerial Baiting and Post-Baiting   62
      Procedures
   c. Endangered Species Label Precautions   63

3. Rangeland and Cropland: Prairie Dogs   64

   a. Bait Concentration Levels   64
   b. Use Supervision   64
   c. Precontrol Survey for the   64
      Black-footed Ferret
   d. Endangered Species Label Precautions   65

4. Rangeland, Cropland, and Non-agricultural   65
   Sites Except Around Ships and Buildings:
   Other Rodents

   a. Bait Concentration Levels   65
   b. Endangered Species Label Precautions   66

5. Pocket Gophers   66

5. Use In and Around Ships and Buildings: 66
   Norway Rat, Roof Rat, and House Mice

VI. Bibliography   67

Appendix A

Executive Summary

The Rebuttable Presumption Against Registration (RPAR)
notice for Compound 1080 (1080) was published in the Federal
Register on December 1, 1976 (41 FR 52792). The presumption
was against the continued registration of all pesticide
products containing 1080 used for rodent control. Compound
1080 was also used for predator control, principally coyotes,
until 1972. At that time the predacidal uses of 1080 were
cancelled. Following a hearing in 1983, EPA determined that
significant new evidence warranted modifications of the 1972
cancellation with respect to the use of 1080 in livestock
protection collars and single lethal dose baits. A
registration for the livestock protection collar was issued
to the Department of the Interior on July 18, 1985.

The RPAR criteria that were determined to have been met
for the rodenticidal uses of 1080 were 1) lack of emergency
treatment, 2) acute toxicity to mammals and birds, and 3)
significant reduction in populations of nontarget organisms
and fatalities to members of endangered species.

Position Document 2/3 (PD 2/3) detailing the Agency's
proposed decision for concluding the RPAR was issued in June,
1983. In PD 2/3 the major actions proposed by the Agency
were the modification in the terms and conditions of use of
1080 to control ground squirrels, prairie dogs and meadow
mice and the denial of the use of 1080 to control several
other species of field rodents. A Federal Register notice
soliciting public comments on PD 2/3 was published on
November 4, 1983 (48 FR 50935). The Agency received comments
on the PD 2/3 from state and county governments, individual
ranchers and farmers, the U.S. Department of Agriculture,
and the Scientific Advisory Panel. All of the comments have
been evaluated and the information has been used in the
development of the Agency's final decision presented in this
document.

The principal use of 1080 is for the control of field
rodents. It is available for this use in the following four
states: California, Colorado, Nevada and Oregon. California
uses over 80% of the 1080 used as a field rodenticide, with
the bulk of the use for the control of ground squirrels.
There are no Federal registrations for any field rodent uses
of 1080, except for a "Special Local Needs" registration
granted under § 24(c) of FIFRA to one county in Oregon.
There is one Federally registered technical product that
contains a use for 1080 to control certain rodents in and
around ships and buildings. California, Colorado and Nevada
use 1080 for field rodent control because they have valid

"intrastate" registrations. Other states who at one time used 1080 for field rodent control relied on the U.S. Department of the Interior's 1080 registration. This registration was withdrawn following an Executive Order prohibiting the use of 1080 on Federal lands.

The Agency has concluded that a variety of regulatory measures can be imposed on current intrastate producers and registrants that will allow the continued use of 1080. A major condition for continued use will be the requirement that all intrastate producers, the § 24(c) registrant and the registrant of technical 1080, submit all data necessary to fully support Federal registration under §3 of FIFRA. Applications for Federal registration or amended registration must be submitted to EPA within 30 days after the publication of the Federal Register notice announcing the availability of PD 4 and the Agency's intent to cancel registrations that do not comply with the terms of the notice, or within 30 days of receipt of written notice to submit an application, which ever occurs later. The data requirements for registration are contained in Appendix A of this document.

In addition to requiring a full complement of data, the Agency is requiring the following regulatory measures to provide protection for endangered and nontarget species while data are generated:

° Utilization of the existing cooperative program between the California Department of Food and Agriculture, Department of Fish and Game, and County Agricultural Commissioners for protection of endangered species in California.

° Direct supervision of 1080 field use by state governmental agency personnel in the range of those endangered species identified in this document.

° Limiting use to Certified Applicators or persons under their direct supervision.

° Changing product labels to include endangered species and nontarget precautions, and revised baiting and post-baiting procedures.

° Lowering 1080 bait concentrations in the range of the California condor and for prairie dog control (which impacts the endangered black-footed ferret).

° Not registering any new product for field rodent control until the data necessary to support Federal registration under § 3 of FIFRA has been submitted and determined to be adequate.

A summary of Agency actions and requirements for ground squirrels, prairie dogs and other rodents is presented at the end of this Executive Summary.

All current uses of 1080 as a rodenticide may be continued under certain conditions, with the possible exception of the use of 1080 in the range of the California condor. Use of 1080 in the range of the condor will be determined prior to January 1, 1986 following discussion with the Office of Endangered Species (OES). The Agency recently received a biological opinion from OES stating that use of the 1080 livestock protection collar in the range of the California condor would jeopardize the continued existence of this species.

The OES opinion emphasized that there are only a few condors in existence and there is uncertainty about the effects of the collar on the condor. Although there are substantial differences in potential 1080 exposure between the livestock protection collar and treated grain bait, the drastic decline in the condor population (OES reported one source estimated 9 to 11 condors in the wild) may require prohibition of 1080 use in the range of the condor until safety data are evaluated by the Agency. If use is permitted in the range of the condor, it will be at a maximum bait concentration of .02% beginning in 1986. This level will be in force until data demonstrating that the .02% level is ineffective are submitted as well as data establishing the lowest effective bait concentration. Bait concentrations higher than .02% will have to be assessed to determine if they pose risks to the condor.

Because of the potential risk to the endangered black-footed ferret, the Agency is requiring that the use of 1080 to control prairie dogs be at a maximum concentration of .02% beginning in 1986. This level will be in force until data demonstrating that the .02% level is ineffective are submitted as well as data establishing the lowest effective bait concentration. Bait concentrations higher than .02% will have to be assessed to determine if they pose risks to the black-footed ferret.

Intrastate producers and the § 24(c) registrant will be able to sell, distribute and use 1080 at current bait concentrations and application rates until field efficacy data are generated, except as noted in the range of the California condor and for control of prairie dogs. Depending on the results of efficacy testing, the Agency may require bait concentrations for additional products to be lowered while other tests necessary to support Federal registration are completed.

As other data for Federal registration are submitted and reviewed by the Agency, additional modifications in the terms and conditions of use may be required. After reviewing the data, the Agency may also determine that some or all uses of a particular product should not be permitted and will cancel registrations or deny application for Federal registration, as appropriate, for those uses in question.

Other states, government agencies, or companies applying for a 1080 registration for field rodent control will be required to generate a full complement of data necessary to support Federal registration prior to the use of 1080. The Agency believes it is necessary that expansion of the use of 1080 to other states be predicated on an adequate data base to support such expansion.

SUMMARY OF ACTIONS

Ground Squirrels- California, Colorado, Nevada, Oregon - all use sites.

°Allow use in 1985 under current label conditions.

°"Call in" intrastate products and require data necessary to support Federal registration under § 3 of FIFRA. Oregon's § 24(c) would also have to meet § 3 data requirements. (See Appendix A).

°Allow products to be used at current bait concentrations and application rates while data are being generated, except in the range of the California condor. If permitted, use after 1985 will be at a maximum bait concentration of .02% in the condor's range unless field efficacy data are submitted demonstrating that the .02% level is not effective as well as data establishing the lowest effective bait concentration. The Agency must determine if higher bait concentrations will impact the condor. A decision on the use of 1080 grain baits in the range of the condor will be made prior to January 1, 1986.

°Applicants for Federal registration and current registrants must begin studies as soon as possible to determine the lowest effective bait concentration.

°Require label changes in baiting and post-baiting procedures, add endangered species and nontarget precautions, and restricted use labeling.

°Withdraw proposed geographic and seasonal use limitations in California. Rely on California state programs approved by EPA.

<u>Prairie Dogs</u>- Colorado - all use sites.

°Allow use during 1985 under current label conditions.

°"Call in" the Colorado intrastate product and require data
necessary to support Federal registration under § 3 of
FIFRA. (See Appendix A).

°Use after 1985 will be at a maximum bait concentration of
.02% unless field efficacy data are submitted demonstrating
that the .02% level is not effective, as well as data
establishing the lowest effective bait concentration.
The Agency must also determine if higher bait concentrations
will impact the black-footed ferret.

°Applicants for Federal registration must begin studies as
soon as possible to determine the lowest effective bait
concentration.

°Allow use after 1985 only if a validated precontrol survey
for the black-footed ferret is approved by the Agency.

°Restrict use to governmental agencies or persons under
the direct supervision of members of governmental agencies.

°Require label changes in baiting and post-baiting procedures,
add endangered species and nontarget precautions, and restricted
use labeling.

<u>Other Rodents</u>- All use sites.

°"Call in" intrastate products and require data necessary
to support Federal registration under § 3 of FIFRA. (See
Appendix A).

°Allow products to be used at current bait concentrations
while data are being generated except in the range of the
California condor. Limitations on 1080 use in the range
of the condor are the same as for ground squirrels.

°Require label changes in baiting and post-baiting procedures,
add endangered species and nontarget precautions, and restricted
use labeling.

°Require that studies to determine the lowest efficacious
bait concentration begin as soon as possible.

°Withdraw proposed seasonal use limitation in California.

<u>Pocket Gophers</u>- All use sites.

°"Call in" intrastate products and require data necessary to support Federal registration under § 3 of FIFRA. (See Appendix A).

°Allow products to be used at current bait concentrations and application rates while data are being generated.

<u>Norway Rat, Roof Rat and House Mice</u>- In and around ships and buildings.

°Allow Uses already on Federal label. Full data base for registration under §3 of FIFRA will be required. (See Appendix A).

I. INTRODUCTION

A. Background

This Position Document 4 (PD 4) concludes the Rebuttable Presumption Against Registration (RPAR) process for sodium monofluoroacetate, commonly called "Compound 1080." Compound 1080 (1080) is currently used as a rodenticide on rangelands, croplands, and nonagricultural sites. Prior to 1972, 1080 was also used for predator control, principally for coyotes. In 1972 the predacidal uses of 1080 were cancelled. This RPAR document addresses only the rodenticidal uses of 1080.

Following a hearing in 1983, EPA determined that significant new evidence warranted modifications of the 1972 cancellation with respect to the use of 1080 in livestock protection collars and single lethal dose baits. Applications for registration of 1080 livestock protection collars are pending before the Agency.

Before 1080 was cancelled for predator control, the Federal registrations for the field rodent uses of 1080 were maintained by the U.S. Fish and Wildlife Service (FWS), U.S. Department of the Interior. Following EPA's cancellation of 1080 as a predacide, Executive Order 11643 was issued, which prohibited the use of 1080 on Federal lands. As a result of this order, the FWS withdrew all their 1080 Federal registrations. In most states, ranchers used the FWS product for control of field rodents and the FWS' withdrawal of its registration resulted in 1080 not being available for this use in those states.

In addition to the FWS registration, three states, California, Colorado and Nevada, had intrastate products containing 1080 registered for field rodent control. Intrastate products are products that may be used only within the state in which they were produced. They are not, however, the same as "special local needs" registrations issued under the authority of § 24(c) of FIFRA. Prior to 1972, EPA did not have authority to regulate products whose manufacture and use were confined solely to one state, i.e. intrastate products. The 1972 amendments to FIFRA expanded EPA's authority to include these products. In 1975 the Agency required that registrants of all intrastate products submit an application indicating their intent to seek Federal registration when asked to do so by EPA. Government agencies in California, Colorado and Nevada had existing intrastate products and filed an application with EPA. EPA allowed all intrastate registrants who filed an acceptable application to continue to use their products until "called in " for Federal registration. To date, none of the 1080 intrastate products has been "called in" for Federal registration.

Current intrastate registrations include 46 in California, three in Nevada, and one in Colorado. There is one § 24(c) registration, which was issued for one county in Oregon in 1981, solely for the control of ground squirrels. There is only one product registered under §3 of FIFRA. This is a technical product used for formulating 1080 end use products. The technical product also contains directions for end use for the control of Norway rats, roof rats, and house mice in and around ships and buildings. The product may be used to control these rodents only by bonded certified commercial applicators.

Estimated annual usage of compound 1080 bait was 610,600 pounds for 1977 (approximately 600 lbs. of active ingredient). Of the total 1080 usage, 75% is for ground squirrel control and 7% for prairie dog control. The remaining uses are for the control of meadow mice, deer mice, wood rat, cotton rat, chipmunks and several other rodent species. California used 83% of the total 1080 used, Colorado 12% and Nevada and Oregon 5%. California indicated in their PD 2/3 comments that annual usage was approximately 100,000 lbs. of bait, which would indicate a considerable reduction in usage from 1977.

Compound 1080 is formulated in baits of grain, rolled oats, or chopped greens for crop and range rodents, and in water bait stations serviced by pest control operators to control commensal rodents. Tull Chemical, in Oxford, Alabama, is the sole U.S. producer of 1080. Compound 1080 is not imported.

B. Position Document 1 (PD 1)

The RPAR notice for compound 1080 was published in the Federal Register of December 1, 1976 (41 FR 52792). The RPAR criteria that were determined to have been met or exceeded for the uses of compound 1080 are: 1) lack of emergency treatment, 2) acute toxicity to mammals and birds, and 3) significant reduction in populations of nontarget organisms and fatalities to members of endangered species. The reasons for the determination were explained in detail in the RPAR notice and accompanying Position Document 1 (PD 1).

In PD 1, the lack of emergency human treatment criterion was based on the following reasons:

- once a sufficiently large dose of compound 1080 is absorbed into the blood stream, the victim will inevitably die.
- symptoms of compound 1080 poisoning may not occur until after a total fatal dose has been absorbed into the blood stream.
- current compound 1080 labels do not specifically prohibit use around domestic dwellings where exposure to children is likely; and

- monoacetin, potentially the most effective medi-
  cation for compound 1080 poisoning, is not available in a pharmaceutical grade.

The acute toxicity criterion was based on a determination
that nontarget mammals and birds are likely to consume lethal
quantities of compound 1080 bait. EPA based its determination
that the significant reduction in nontarget organism populations
criterion was met primarily on acute oral toxicity data. These
data suggested that a risk to various wildlife species, through
direct ingestion of 1080 treated bait, could reasonably be
expected. A lethal quantity could also be consumed indirectly
by eating a rodent poisoned with 1080. Compound 1080 LD_{50}
values are not available for many of the nontarget species which
EPA suspected could be affected. Risk to such nontarget
species was based on available toxicity values of target and
nontarget species.

The criterion for endangered species was supported by a
laboratory study that demonstrated a hazard to the endangered
San Joaquin kit fox from secondary poisoning as well as the
available toxicity data. In the secondary hazard study, a
kangaroo rat was killed with a quantity of compound 1080
that could be consumed by the rat by ingesting grain bait
treated with compound 1080. A desert kit fox, a subspecies
of kit fox closely related to the endangered San Joaquin kit
fox, was fatally poisoned by eating the kangaroo rat.
(Schitoskey, 1975)

C. Summary of Actions Proposed in PD 2/3

The Agency issued another Position Document (PD 2/3)
in June, 1983. Notice of the PD 2/3 was published in the
Federal Register on November 4, 1983 (48 FR 50935). In
PD 2/3, the Agency responded to comments received in response
to PD 1, analyzed the risks and benefits of each 1080 use
and each regulatory option, and proposed regulatory actions.
The proposed actions were designed to reduce risks to the
point where they would be exceeded by the benefits of use.
In some instances, this necessitated proposals to deny
applications for registration; denial is appropriate rather
than cancellation because the products involved were intrastate
products and not federally registered. A summary of proposed
actions by site and pest follows.

Rangeland and pasture use.

    ground squirrels- modification of the terms and conditions of
                      registration
    prairie dogs   - modification of the terms and conditions of
                      registration

```
pocket gophers  - no action
chipmunks       - denial of applications
cotton rats     - denial of applications
deer mice       - denial of applications
kangaroo rats   - denial of applications
meadow mice     - denial of applications
```

Cropland use.

```
ground squirrels- modification of the terms and conditions of
                    registration
prairie dogs    - modification of the terms and conditions of
                    registration
meadow mice     - modification of the terms and conditions of
                    registration
pocket gophers  - no action
Norway rats     - denial of applications
cotton rats     - denial of applications
wood rats       - denial of applications
```

Use in and around buildings and ships.

```
Norway rats     - no action
roof rats       - no action
house mice      - no action
```

Use on other nonagricultural sites.

```
ground squirrels- modification of the terms and conditions of
(on ditch banks,  registration
levees, canals,
and earthen dams)
chipmunks       - denial of applications
cotton rats     - denial of applications
Norway rats     - denial of applications
kangaroo rats   - denial of applications
wood rats       - denial of applications
deer mice       - denial of applications
meadow mice     - denial of applications
pocket gophers  - no action
```

The modifications of the terms and conditions of registration included reductions in active ingredient concentration, uniform baiting and post baiting procedures, and seasonal, geographical and other special restrictions for the protection of endangered species.

In PD 2/3, the Agency determined that the lack of emergency human treatment criterion, the acute toxicity criterion, the significant reduction in nontarget organism populations and endangered species criterion had not been rebutted.

In addition, for the criterion for endangered species, the Agency used the evaluations of the Office of Endangered Species (OES). OES was asked to identify any endangered species that might be exposed to 1080 from rodent control programs. OES noted 12 such species:

San Joaquin kit fox (<u>Vulpes</u> <u>macrotis</u> <u>mutica</u>)
Black-footed ferret (<u>Mustela</u> <u>nigripes</u>)
Morro Bay kangaroo rat (<u>Dipodomys</u> <u>heermanni</u> <u>morroensis</u>)
Salt marsh harvest mouse (<u>Reithrodonotomys</u> <u>raviventris</u>)
California condor (<u>Gymnogyps</u> <u>californianus</u>)
Aleutian Canada goose (<u>Branta</u> <u>canadensis</u> <u>leucopareia</u>)
Bald eagle (<u>Haliaeetus</u> <u>leucocephalus</u>)
Arctic peregrine falcon (<u>Falco</u> <u>peregrinus</u> <u>tundrius</u>)
American peregrine falcon (<u>Falco</u> <u>pregrinus</u> <u>anatum</u>)
Santa Barbara song sparrow (<u>Melospiza</u> <u>melodia</u> <u>graminea</u>)
San Clemente sage sparrow (<u>Amphispiza</u> <u>belli</u> <u>clementeae</u>)
San Clemente loggerhead shrike (<u>Lanius</u> <u>ludovcianus</u> <u>mearnsi</u>)

Of the 12, OES concluded that exposure to 1080 under current label conditions was not likely to jeopardize the continued existence of 7 species. They also concluded that new label restrictions would minimize exposure and adequately protect the remaining 5 endangered species. These species were: the California condor, San Joaquin kit fox, black-footed ferret, Morro Bay kangaroo rat and the salt marsh harvest mouse (FWS correspondence, July 21, 1978). The Agency concurred with the OES assessment, but expanded it to include additional safeguards for the Aleutian Canada goose.

The Agency's concern about endangered species, especially the San Joaquin kit fox and the black-footed ferret, was supported by the fact that nontarget species had been killed by feeding on animals poisoned by 1080.

D. Organization of Position Document 4

Chapter II of this document presents the public comments on the Agency's PD 2/3 risk assessment and details the Agency's response to these comments. Chapter III discusses benefits in the same manner as risks are discussed in Chapter II. Chapter IV summarizes the Agency's proposed regulatory actions in PD 2/3, presents the public comments on these proposed actions, and details the Agency's response to the comments. Chapter V presents the Agency's regulatory decision.

II. Comments and Agency Response on the PD 2/3 Risk Assessment

The purpose of this chapter is to review and evaluate comments submitted to the Agency in response to PD 2/3 and to revise, as appropriate, the determination of risks used to reach the risk/benefit decisions on the rodenticidal uses of 1080.

Comments regarding risk associated with the use of 1080 are organized into sections:

    A) General comments on risk assessment
    B) Comments on lack of emergency treatment criterion
    C) Comments on acute toxicity to mammals and birds criterion
    D) Comments on significant adverse effects on populations
        of nontarget organisms criterion
    E) Comments on endangered species criterion

A. General Comments on Risk Assessment

The Scientific Advisory Panel, Wyoming Department of Agriculture and the Montana Department of Agriculture made general comments on the risk assessment presented in PD 2/3.

1. Scientific Advisory Panel (SAP)

The SAP commented that there was very little definitive data to support the contention that 1080 presented a serious hazard to non-target species, including endangered or threatened species. The Panel found that the rationale for the action proposed in PD 2/3, especially the reduction in bait concentration to 0.02 percent and reduction of the rate of application to 4 lbs./acre was not adequately explained or justified. The Panel also noted that the actions proposed in PD 2/3 were not, in general, well supported.

Although the Agency agrees with the Panel that there are data gaps with 1080, as noted several times in PD 2/3, the Agency also believes there are enough data available to provide a basis for concern about potential risks to nontargets, especially endangered species. In particular the Agency relies on the Hegdal (1979) study, and on other field and laboratory studies demonstrating the toxicity of 1080 to various rodent and nontarget species.

Furthermore, as clearly required under FIFRA, the responsibility for establishing the safety and, if appropriate, efficacy of a pesticide product rests with the registrant and not with EPA. A complete data base for 1080 has not been generated in large part because of the registration status of the 1080 field rodenticide use products. As noted in the Introduction, all of the current 1080 products bearing field rodent uses are intrastate products and have never been subject to the data requirements for Federal registration under § 3 of FIFRA. Existing intrastate products will be "called in" for Federal registration and new applicants for 1080 registration will have to submit data to support registration prior to the use of 1080. These actions will ensure that the potential risk concerns of the Agency are addressed and will provide a more complete data base to determine if 1080 can be used without unreasonable adverse effects on the environment.

2. Wyoming Department of Agriculture

In its comments the Wyoming Department of Agriculture asked a number of questions:

1) What type of investigations of unreasonable adverse effects were made to support PD 2/3?

2) Was there a significant effect that triggered the issuance of PD 1 in 1976, and since 1976, what data are available to evaluate the effect of reduced 1080 bait concentrations?

3) What sociological study was produced by EPA to support its regulatory action in PD 2/3?

4) What studies have been produced by EPA on the conversion of prime farm land to other uses not compatible with prime farm land objectives when 1080 rodenticides are not available?

In response to the first two questions the Agency has established RPAR criteria that it believes are indicators of potential risk. The criteria exceeded were identified and discussed in both PD 1 and PD 2/3. It is important to recognize that EPA is not limited to taking regulatory action only on the demonstrated occurrence of adverse effects.

EPA did not generate any sociological studies or evaluations regarding the loss of prime farm land because the Agency did not believe its proposed 1080 regulatory actions would cause the impact suggested by Wyoming. Other pesticides are available for field rodent control and Wyoming and other applicants have been free to pursue registration of 1080 for rodent control under § 3 of FIFRA.

Wyoming also commented that "EPA has repeatedly and arbitrarily denied Wyoming's registration applications for special local need (Intrastate) use of 1080 for field rodent control purposes under 162.17 of EPA regulations (Ref 2) (letters)."

The two letters (telegrams from EPA to the Wyoming Department of Agriculture) submitted by Wyoming in support of this contention do not present a clear picture of what transpired. One telegram stated that EPA was not accepting Wyoming's application for two 1080 products under the intrastate program. This same telegram also referenced recent court action vacating an injunction against enforcement of EPA's suspension and cancellation action against the predacide uses of 1080. Apparently the Wyoming intrastate products contained predacide uses as well as field rodent uses and were not acceptable for inclusion in the intrastate program.

Wyoming and other states interested in obtaining or expanding 1080 use may submit applications for Experimental Use Permits to generate data necessary for registration or otherwise provide such data. The Agency will give such requests full and fair consideration.

3. Montana Department of Agriculture

Montana commented that PD 2/3 did not reflect their use experience with 1080 in controlling Columbian ground squirrels and that data collected from this use should be considered in the Agency's 1080 decision.

The Agency did not address Montana's use of 1080 to control Columbian ground squirrels because this use has been permitted under the emergency exemption procedures of §18 of FIFRA. Emergency exemption uses are not registered uses and are issued only in unusual circumstances. In addition, the Columbian ground squirrel is not a pest species in the four states using 1080 to control squirrels and Montana's data could not be extrapolated to other ground squirrel species. Montana will be required to seek Federal registration for this use and the data generated in their use experience will be evaluated as part of the registration process.

B. Lack of Emergency Treatment

1. Agency Position in PD 2/3

In PD 2/3, the Agency determined that the presumption against registration for 1080, based on a lack of emergency treatment, was not rebutted because possible antidotes were either unavailable commercially or were of unproven effectiveness against a lethal dose. The Agency did note that early first aid treatment of small ingested amounts can be effective.

The Agency reviewed the available accident history with 1080 since its use began in 1946. The record showed several poisoning incidents involving humans (adults and children), and domestic animals, most of which occurred in the early years of 1080 use. The Agency also noted that the accidents were mostly associated with use in and around buildings and that current label instructions and restrictions on use made it unlikely that humans and pets would now be exposed to 1080.

2. Comments on PD 2/3

One commenter, Montana, observed that there may be an adequate emergency treatment for 1080 poisoning in humans in the future. Specifically, they remarked that a pharmaceutical grade of monoacetin, identified in PD 2/3 as a possible treatment, may become available. This would be desirable and the Agency urges the development of effective antidotes or emergency treatment.

The same commenter also observed that there is no record of any human fatalities or poisonings with 1080 from field rodent use in over 35 years of use. Other State regulatory officials have also noted the lack of human poisoning or fatalities from the field rodent uses of 1080.

3. Agency Response

The comments submitted regarding the Agency's concern about the lack of emergency treatment have not persuaded the Agency to alter its position. Possible antidotes either are not available or have not been proven effective against a lethal dose of 1080. However, as noted in PD 2/3 most of the reported human poisoning incidents with 1080 have occurred with the commensal rodent use rather than the field rodent use and several measures have reduced risks considerably. These measures include:

° upgrading of the label instructions for use.

° classification as a restricted use pesticide and its subsequent use only by certified pest control operators or governmental agency personnel.

° prohibition of use in occupied dwellings.

° placement of bait in tamper proof bait boxes.

° the generally restrictive state regulations governing the use of 1080 as a commensal rodenticide.

The Agency believes for the field rodenticide uses that the risks regarding the criterion of lack of emergency treatment are less than the risks for commensal rodent use based on:

° the accident record, which indicates few if any confirmed human poisonings,

° the strict use requirements and safeguards imposed by the states, particularly California, where over 80% of 1080 rodenticides are used, and

° classification as a restricted use pesticide and use only by certified applicators or persons under their direct supervision.

Notwithstanding the lack of a proven, effective, available emergency treatment regimen, the Agency is proposing no additional regulatory actions based on this criterion because of the risk reduction measures now in place.

C. Acute Toxicity to Mammals and Birds

1. Agency Position in PD 2/3

In PD 2/3 the Agency reported the acute oral toxicity of 1080 to numerous species of mammals, amphibians, and birds. The median lethal single oral dosages expressed as mg of 1080 per kg animal weight (LD_{50}'s) ranged from 0.056 mg/kg for nutria to 60 mg/kg for the opossum. The Agency noted that even though a 1000-fold range in susceptibility was indicated to exist between species, all species listed were very sensitive to the toxic action of 1080 and exceeded the RPAR criterion for acute toxicity.

Among vertebrates tested, available data indicated that mammals are generally the most sensitive, notably nutria, cotton rat, kit fox, and other members of the dog and cat families.

2. Comments on PD 2/3

Wyoming observed that acute toxicity data are not meaningful unless discussed in conjunction with exposure data. The California Department of Food and Agriculture (CDFA) noted that "It is a scientifically accepted fact that toxicity and risk do not go hand in hand and that there are many other factors involved." CDFA believes that feeding behavior, food preferences, and aversive conditioning to toxicants were not given due consideration by EPA. Montana commented that the risks to birds, mammals and endangered species are often evaluated from LD50 data of biologically similar or closely related species. They observed that this may be inaccurate since available LD50 data shows considerable variation in susceptability to 1080. Montana also questioned the reliability of present LD50 data.

Another commenter (Defenders of Wildlife) stated that 1080 is more toxic to canine and feline species than to rodents, and that no rodenticide which poses greater risks to nontarget species than to target pests should be used.

3. Agency Response

The Agency concurs in principal with the comments concerning the relationship between toxicity and hazard, but notes that acute toxicity data is an important indicator of potential risk. The Agency notes that available data indicate a range of sensitivity to 1080 among related species and also recognizes that the reliability of some of the LD50 data may be questionable. However, the Agency's conclusion from these facts, is that while there is uncertainty in predicting risks to untested species the available data suggest that 1080 presents risks that may be high to certain nontarget species. Because of these uncertainties, the Agency is requiring data that will provide a better understanding of these risks.

Regarding the comment from Defenders of Wildlife, the Agency agrees that it would be desirable for all rodenticides to be more toxic to rodents than to any nontarget species. However, as noted in the preceeding paragraphs, toxicity is not the sole component of risk. As the Agency reviews data for registration and the nature of nontarget risk becomes clearer, additional risk reduction measures may be required.

D. Significant Adverse Effects on Populations of Nontarget Organisms

1. Agency's Position in PD 2/3

a. General

In PD 2/3, the risk assessment was based on the use of 1080 to control ground squirrels. For other pest species there were insufficient data to form the basis of a complete risk assessment and no further data have been submitted. Therefore, the Agency assumes, as it did in PD 2/3, that the risks posed by the use of 1080 on pests other than ground squirrels are analagous to those risks from the ground squirrel use.

b. Direct Risks to Nontarget Species

As noted in PD 2/3, the presence of 1080 treated bait in the field may pose a risk to nontarget vertebrate species that may feed on bait and such feeding may result in significant population reductions in the nontarget species. The Agency relied on the results of the Hegdal field study as an indicator of potential direct risks to nontarget species.

The Hegdal study evaluated the hazards to wildlife associated with aerial 1080 baiting for California ground squirrels. The study was conducted in Tulare County, California, in the eastern foothills of the San Joaquin Valley. The study monitored a large-scale (60,000 acres) operational baiting program conducted by the Tulare County Agricultural Commission. Ground squirrel populations were reduced about 85% following baiting.

The results of the study showed that 1) avian species were not severely impacted and 2) direct effects on rabbits and nontarget rodents were more substantial than for birds.

c. Indirect Risks to Nontarget Species

Several laboratory studies and the Hegdal field study indicate that secondary poisoning of animals (poisoning of animals which eat a victim of direct exposure) can readily occur with 1080.

One study was conducted by Tucker (1965-72) with domestic ferrets (Mustela putorius). Ferrets were fed the intact bodies of albino rats which had been stomach-tubed with 1080 two hours prior to feeding. Ferrets eating rats containing dosages of 2 mg/kg or less exhibited strong poisoning symptoms while dosages of 8 mg/kg and above were fatal to ferrets.

In a similar experiment by Tucker with <u>Peromyscus</u> sp. and ferrets, ferrets that ingested mice that had been stomach-tubed to contain one mg 1080 per kg of ferret weight died. Based on this study, the Agency concluded that if as little as 1 gram of a 2 oz/100 lb. (0.125%) bait were ingested directly by a ferret, it would most likely be lethal. The Agency also concluded that if 1080-poisoned prairie dogs were fed upon by black-footed ferrets, a similar hazard could exist.

Hedgal, Gatz and Fite (1980) fed Richardson's ground squirrels that had died from eating known amounts of 1080 bait to coyotes with subsequent fatalities. Coyotes that died had consumed squirrels that had eaten the equivalent of 0.45, 0.47 and 0.75 mg 1080/kg of coyote. Coyotes that survived had consumed ground squirrels that had eaten the equivalent of 0.14, 0.28 and 0.35 mg/kg. Therefore, these results suggest coyotes (LD_{50} .12 mg/kg) must consume about 4 times their LD_{50} in poisoned ground squirrels before they are killed. Apparently the 1080 in the primary consumer is detoxified; through metabolic processes or other mechanisms, possibly a dilution effect from the feed.

The Hegdal study was also used to assess secondary risks to nontarget species. As reported in PD 2/3, secondary hazards to raptors and mammalian predators were evaluated by attaching transmitters to 24 raptors (red-tailed hawks, turkey vultures, a golden eagle, great horned owls, a screech owl, common ravens, a common crow), and 42 mammalian predators (bobcats, coyotes, gray fox, badgers, striped skunks, raccoons, and opossum) and monitoring their movements before, during, and after treatment. While the fate of many of these animals was not determined, five of the six radio-equipped coyotes and three of the ten radio-equipped bobcats (one bobcat was emaciated, possibly the result of a trap injury), were found dead after treatment. Three dead striped skunks (not radio-equipped) and a coyote (not radio-equipped) were also found dead after treatment. One striped skunk contained 1080 residues. No other treatment-related mortalities were indicated among the remaining radio-equipped birds or mammals. Also, monitoring of 58 active raptor nests indicated no treatment-related mortalities.

Several aspects of those observations on coyotes and bobcats were relevant:

° While the carcasses showed symptoms typical of 1080 poisoning and the general circumstances make it

highly likely that death was caused by 1080, any
residues of 1080 were below the level of detection.

° Most of the animals died in locations where their
discovery would have been unlikely had they not been
equipped with transmitters.

° While the samples are small, the data suggest that
1080 presents a high risk of secondary poisoning
to coyotes and to a lesser degree the bobcat. The
data also suggest a potential for impacts on other
mammalian scavengers.

° A year later, coyotes appeared to have returned to
pretreatment levels.

The available evidence led the Agency to the conclusion
that secondary poisoning from 1080 can be expected, although
there is considerable uncertainty in quantifying the risk.

The Agency concluded in PD 2/3 that the use of 1080 to
control ground squirrels posed a secondary risk to local populations of predators. The magnitude of the risk varies with
details of the control program and the status of the nontarget population and may extend to regional populations,
however, the Agency believed the data was insufficient to
support denial of this use.

d. Community Level Impacts

In PD 2/3, the Agency discussed in some detail another
concern regarding the potential effects of non-target predator
mortality resulting from ground squirrel control programs.
This concern was the predator-prey relationship, and the effects
that might result from severely altering the population of a
predator species. The Agency noted that there are many examples
of how the use of pesticides to control insects has created new
pest situations by killing the predators and parasites that
formerly kept potential pests in check. The Agency believed
that the possible similar relationships between ground squirrels
and their predators deserved consideration. The Agency recognized
that while there was little basis for believing that predators
alone could prevent the development of economically damaging
densities of ground squirrels, it was reasonable to suspect
that predators could serve a useful function in population
management.

There is substantial evidence that mammalian predator
populations, while they seldom may be capable of reducing a
high prey population, are capable of suppressing low populations

of microtines and lagomorphs and retarding their recovery (Todd, 1980). Support for this position is found in studies of voles in California (Pearson, 1966, 1971), jackrabbits in Utah (Wagner and Stoddart, 1972) and rabbits in Australia (Myers, 1980). To the extent that similar relationships may exist between carnivores and ground squirrels, it follows that the use of a toxicant that kills substantial numbers of carnivores at the very time that the populations of the target pests have been reduced to low levels will have the effect of enabling the target population to recover at a more rapid rate. The circumstances under which predation by carnivores and raptors can effectively suppress low populations of ground squirrels needs to be determined, but the Agency suggested that the disruption of natural regulatory mechanisms is an adverse effect beyond the immediate secondary mortality.

Although the Hegdal study suggested the likelihood of high mortality to predators, particularly the coyote, the Agency noted that a year after the Hegdal study, coyote population indexes had returned to prestudy levels.

e. Relation of Bait Formulations to Risks

In PD 2/3 the Agency discussed rates of application, concentrations of 1080 in the bait, and methods of application and how these variables may affect risks to nontarget organisms and efficacy in reducing target species. The Agency noted that, unfortunately, there is a paucity of information that would directly permit a very accurate assessment of these relationships. However, the Agency concluded that available data suggested that risks might be reduced by lowering the bait concentration without reducing efficacy.

The Agency believed that given the LD_{50}, the size of the animals and the concentration of 1080 in the bait, the amount of bait required to kill an animal could be estimated. For target species, a practical lethal "dose" would be an LD_{95} for the largest individuals in the population. For nontarget species, risk may be based on an LD_{50} for an average animal or some more stringent criterion for populations of great concern, such as endangered species.

A major question from the standpoint of both efficacy and secondary risk concerns the amount of bait normally consumed by the target animals. In an area intentionally over-baited by hand, Sibley (1966) estimated that the average squirrel found dead had consumed about 100 grains of bait. He did not indicate his methods or assumptions and the accuracy of this estimate cannot be assessed. Based on Agency interpretation of data developed by Marsh (1967), the Agency concluded that the average squirrel may consume 200 grains of bait if this is applied when there is one squirrel per active burrow. The Agency noted that if 200 grains is an expected dose, secondary risks will depend on residual toxicity of the bait, the lethal dose for a scavenger, and how many squirrels a scavenger is likely to eat. Relying on published LD_{50} values of uncertain accuracy and an approximation of average body weight for nontarget species in California, the Agency calculated the number of squirrels consuming 200 kernels of various 1080 bait concentrations required to produce a carnivore LD50, assuming 75 percent detoxification. These calculations indicated that at a 1080 bait concentration of 0.1 percent a coyote LD50 would be less than 1 squirrel while the LD 50 for a kit fox would be approximately 0.3 squirrels.

The Agency concluded, therefore that both the coyote and kit fox are clearly at great risk from applications of 0.05% to 0.1% formulations if they feed on dead squirrels. The Agency also believed these estimates were reasonably consistent with the observations of Hegdal in his 1979 study and the internal consistency provided the Agency confidence that its risk assessment was reasonable. Using the mink as a surrogate for the black-footed ferret, it appeared to the Agency that there was virtually no margin of safety under similar patterns of baiting. A thorough detailed discussion of the Agency's calculations and assumptions was presented in PD 2/3.

The Agency concluded that broadcast application of 0.08% and 0.1% bait poses equal or greater secondary risks to carnivores than hand application of 0.05% bait. It was also suggested that secondary risks may be reduced by lowering the concentration of 1080 in the bait.

2. Comments on PD 2/3

The comments in this section have been grouped by major topic. These topics include comments on the Hegdal study, predator prey relationships, and relationship of bait formulation to risk.

a. The Hegdal Study (1979)

As noted several times in PD 2/3, the 1979 Hegdal study was used to assess the potential risk to non-target species from 1080 ground squirrel control programs. The California Department of Food and Agriculture (CDFA) offered several comments on the Hegdal study. They believed that the study has many serious flaws, several of which make some of the data and subsequent conclusions invalid or highly questionable. CDFA cautions that the decision on ground squirrel control has important economic and environmental consequences and basing conclusions on a single study involving highly questionable research practices is suspect. The major points that CDFA raised concerning the Hegdal study were:

° A failure by the Agency to consider that the attachment of radio transmitters and collars on some species may alter the behavior, particularly feeding behavior, of the monitored species. This may result in a tagged animal feeding more extensively on carrion or sick animals than it would normally. CDFA cited several studies demonstrating that the attachment of radio transmitters alters behavior.

° CDFA believes the above point is especially pertinent to
  the Hegdal study because researchers trapped predators
  up to and including the night before the baiting commenced.
  A number of predators had very little time to recover from
  soreness or injury incurred during trapping or time to
  adjust to the radio-collars. CDFA believed that the
  trauma resulting from being trapped, tranquilized, radio-
  tagged and released at the same time dead squirrels became
  available, increased the likelihood that these animals
  were prone to feeding on carrion instead of seeking live
  prey.

° CDFA notes that there was no control group trapped outside
  the 1080 baiting area to determine mortality resulting from
  trap injuries or the carrying of transmitters.

° CDFA believed that the practice of luring predators to
  traps with fetid scent rather than with live prey biased
  the predator sample in that predators with a predisposition
  to decomposing flesh were attracted to the traps and
  subsequently used in the study. CDFA believes this factor
  would explain the high mortality of coyotes and bobcats
  (assuming that all deaths were attributable to 1080, a
  conclusion that CDFA does not believe is supported by the
  study).

° CDFA believes that the analytical results failing to
  identify 1080 in the tissue of many animals supports the
  contention that the radios may have contributed to the
  deaths of some animals.

° CDFA questioned the usefulness of the study finding that
  necropsies of dead animals generally showed symptoms similar
  to those indicated for 1080 intoxication. CDFA notes that
  the pathology of 1080 killed animals is often inconclusive.
  Without analytical confirmation that 1080 is present in a
  carcass, the necropsy alone carries little weight. CDFA
  further notes that even with positive analytical data, there
  is no assurance at very low levels that some other factor
  may not be the cause of death.

° CDFA also questioned the Agency's statement that the Hegdal
data suggested that 50 to 100% of the local coyote
population and from zero to 50% of the local bobcat
population may be killed from 1080 ground squirrel control
programs in similar circumstances. CDFA noted that of
seven coyotes tagged, one died before treatment, one
survived, and there is no conclusive evidence that the
other five died from 1080. They also note that even if
the five post treatment deaths were attributed to 1080,
the percentage kill would be five out of seven or 71%
of the population sampled. A similar comment on the
bobcat fatalities was noted with CDFA commenting that
20% not 50% would be the upper limit since two of ten
bobcats were killed. (CDFA apparently did not include
the third dead bobcat since it had an injured leg and
was emaciated).

b. Predator Prey Relationship

CDFA did not share the Agency's concern regarding the
possible adverse effects of predator population suppression.
CDFA believes the Agency has failed to consider a major difference
between mammalian prey and predators and insect prey and
predators. CDFA points out that many insect predators are
species-specific in selecting prey, while coyotes and bobcats
are opportunistic in selecting prey. Montana also noted
that predators are opportunistic and that if one prey species
becomes less abundant, predators will switch to more easily
obtainable prey. CDFA noted that in many mammalian predator-prey
relationships the number of prey has a greater influence on
the number of predators than the reverse. They further note
that there is evidence that predation probably stimulates
reproduction in the prey species and keeps the prey population
at a higher sustained level than if no predation existed at
all (Howard 1974).

CDFA contends that there is no evidence that any incidental
loss of predators such as coyotes or bobcats during rodent
control with 1080 has resulted in a predator-prey imbalance or
that the disruption of natural regulatory mechanisms has resulted
in adverse effects beyond secondary mortality in the immediate
area.

The Montana Department of Agriculture (Montana) also believes it is unrealistic and at odds with field observations that predators can maintain a prey species at a low level. They also note that population reductions of such species may be masked or magnified by other population trends unrelated to 1080 use and that populations of nontarget predators, especially coyotes, recover rapidly.

Defenders of Wildlife stated that 1080 may cause local depletions in populations of nontarget species, specifically coyotes by secondary poisoning and that such depletions, if frequent, may disrupt entire biotic communities. The same commenter stated that local bobcat populations would be threatened by use of 1080 particularly in light of trapping of bobcats.

c. Relationship of Bait Formulation to Risk

CDFA commented that the Agency overlooked several factors that influence the formulation of effective rodenticide baits. Some of these factors include:

° The LD100 in a free feeding situation.
° How much an animal consumes in a free feeding situation.
° How quickly symptoms occur to cause the target species to stop feeding.
° The kind of bait used.
° The type of carrier used.
° Consideration of toxicant loss during storage, slough-off losses in the storage sack, loss because of light rains.

CDFA believes that knowing only the LD95 and weight of the animal in formulating bait concentration invites the development of resistance problems. CDFA does note that an optimum bait concentration for 1080 can be determined by a series of laboratory feedings and subsequent field tests.

CDFA also takes issue with the Agency's assumptions regarding the amount of bait consumed by a ground squirrel, an important factor in estimating secondary poisoning risks. The 200 kernels per squirrel average used by the Agency is regarded as too high by CDFA and they point to Sibley's study (1966), which showed that dead squirrels consumed about 100 kernels of bait and further noted that Sibley intentionally overbaited.

CDFA also contended that there were no data to support the Agency's assumption that broadcast application of 0.08 percent and 0.1 percent bait posed a equal or greater secondary risk to carnivores than hand application of 0.05 percent bait.

CDFA believes that the evidence does not show that aerial broadcasting presents a greater secondary risk to any carnivore.

d. Other Comments

Several commenters (CDFA, Montana, Wyoming Department of Agriculture) state generally that the data on the effects of 1080 on populations of non-target organisms are incomplete or subject to differing interpretations. They concluded from this that compound 1080 has not been shown to cause significant adverse effects on populations of nontarget organisms.

Several comments were made about the toxic action and other intrinsic characteristics of 1080. For instance, commenters disagreed with the Agency that 1080 is uniformly distributed in the bodies of 1080-poisoned animals (CDFA, Wyoming); that it is moderately accumulated from sublethal doses (CDFA); that it has no significant flavor (CDFA); that it induces regurgitation in some species of poisoned animals (CDFA, Wyoming); that 1080 is a fast-acting poison (CDFA, Wyoming).

Three commenters, (CDFA, Montana, Wyoming) argued that laboratory toxicity testing has little relevance to field exposures to 1080 and there is no credible evidence that 1080 affects nontarget populations.

3. Agency Response

a. The Hegdal Study

As noted, the Hegdal field study was a major component of the Agency's risk asessment in PD 2/3. Notwithstanding CDFA's many objections to the conduct of the study and the Agency's conclusions drawn from it, EPA concludes that the study clearly demonstrates secondary poisoning risks from 1080 field rodent control programs. CDFA acknowledges that some coyotes and occasionally even a bobcat may be killed from such programs.

The Agency also recognizes that trap injuries, placement of radio transmitters and use of carrion to lure test animals may have affected the results to some degree and that a control group would have been useful for comparison. However, the Hegdal study was a major cooperative effort involving EPA, U.S. Fish and Wildlife Service and California regulatory personnel. Efforts were made to safeguard the integrity of the study and the Agency notes that carrion lures are commonly used in studies to attract coyotes. Further, there are no data to suggest that a substantial portion of the coyote population do not eat carrion whenever it is available.

The Agency recognizes that there is always room for improvement in study design and execution, but as CDFA noted in their comments, no study is perfect and faults can be found with any study. The Agency does not believe that the criticism of the study advanced by CDFA detracts from the basic conclusions regarding secondary risk. However, the Agency also recognizes the inappropriateness of relying solely or too heavily on one study.

The Hegdal study confirmed the sensitivity of coyotes, and to a lesser extent bobcats to 1080 from actual field trials. Prior to the Hegdal study there was a sense that actual field mortalities, although they occurred, were not significant. The level of mortality, 5 of 6 tagged coyotes killed, does indicate the potential for significant secondary poisoning effects of this species even when considering the "biases" that CDFA has suggested. The fact that coyotes are secondarily killed by 1080 is evidence in the Agency's opinion to pursue a conservative course in protecting other species, particularly endangered species. As noted previously, coyote sensitivity to 1080 is especially important as an indicator of potential risk to the endangered San Joaquin kit fox and the black-footed ferret.

b. Predator-Prey Relationship

The discussion of predator-prey relationships in PD 2/3 was presented to underscore the complexities that exist in the biotic community. The Agency is not suggesting that the coyote alone can keep ground squirrel populations in check. The Agency also agrees that the coyote/ground squirrel relationship is not comparable in any specific sense to those relationships that exist in the insect community. Nevertheless the Agency does not believe it prudent to totally ignore predator-prey relationships.

Since these relationships are not well understood, the Agency concludes nonselective killing of nontargets is best avoided. As noted in the discussion of the Hegdal study, to achieve this end the Agency is requiring that data be developed to determine if reduced bait concentrations can reduce potential risks.

c. Relationship of Bait Formulation to Risk

CDFA's comments on the factors that influence the formulation of effective rodenticide baits are well taken. EPA acknowledges CDFA and the County Agriculture Commissions expertise in this matter. However, data have not been presented to show that reduced bait concentration levels and application rates will not be efficacious. The Agency concludes it is necessary to establish minimum effective bait concentration and application rates and determine if a reduction in potential hazard to nontarget wildlife will follow.

d. Other Comments

The Agency agrees that many useful data on 1080 and population effects are missing, incomplete or subject to differing interpretations. However, existing data reasonably show the potential for population effects in the coyote and suggest the potential for population effects in other sensitive nontarget species. These risk concerns may be reduced significantly by the use of 1080 at reduced bait concentration and application rates.

The Agency assumes that the purpose of those comments disagreeing with the Agency's characterization of 1080's intrinsic properties was to support the contention that 1080 does not inherently pose any risk of secondary poisoning. The Agency's discussion of the properties of 1080 may be open to differences in interpretation . However, the Hegdal study and available LD50 data indicate that certain measures are necessary to reduce nontarget risk.

The Agency agrees that more extensive field data would be preferrable to extrapolations from laboratory data in estimating risks to nontarget species. In addition, the Agency does not agree that laboratory data has little revelance in risk assessment. In the absence or limited availability of field data, the Agency has relied on laboratory data, existing field data, and reasonable exposure assumptions. The Agency concludes that this risk criterion is not rebutted merely by intrinsic problems of extrapolation between laboratory and field testing.

E. Endangered Species

The Agency's concern over the potential adverse effects on endangered species is an important factor in shaping the regulatory measures discussed in this document. The focus of this concern is to ensure that the use of 1080 to control rodents will not jeopardize the continued existence of any endangered species. Of the endangered species identified by the Fish and Wildlife Service and EPA as species that might be exposed to 1080 from rodent control programs, two are of particular concern. They are the California condor and the black-footed ferret. The reason for the high level of concern for these two species is that their survivability is more tenuous than the other identified endangered species.

A summary of the Agency's risk assessment in PD 2/3, comments, and Agency response on the the California condor, the San Joaquin kit fox, the black-footed ferret, and the Aleutian Canada goose follows. Two other endangered species, the Morro Bay kangaroo rat and the salt marsh harvest mouse, were also identified in PD 2/3 as requiring modifications in the terms and conditions of use, but no comments were received. Many of the risk concerns discussed in Section D. of this chapter, population effects on nontarget organisms, were also important factors in the Agency's determination of risks to endangered species.

1. California Condor

a. Agency Position in PD 2/3

In PD 2/3 the Agency noted the complexity of assessing the risk to condors from exposure to 1080. The key component of 1080 exposure was the extent that condors fed on poisoned ground squirrels and which parts of squirrel carcasses condors consumed. The Agency believed that there was ample evidence that condors will feed on poisoned ground squirrels, however, the extent was not known nor was there any clear indication as to which parts of the squirrel carcass condors will not consume. For purposes of the Agency's risk assessment it assumed that a condor may consume the contents of squirrel cheek pouches and stomach as well as unmetabolized, absorbed 1080.

Utilizing the work of Sibley (1966) on the amount of 1080 treated grain contained in a ground squirrels cheek pouches as a starting point, and making certain "margin of safety" assumptions that took into account existing LD 50 values for the turkey vulture and the interspecific variations in sensitivity to 1080, the Agency estimated that a condor may have to feed on only a few 1080 poisoned squirrels to be at risk. The Agency also expressed concern about consumption of individual squirrels that might contain substantially more 1080 than an "average" squirrel.

The Agency also noted that the condor's current plight was due primarily to its failure to reproduce. The Agency cited certain preliminary data on the effects of 1080 on the testes of birds, which showed that there was no evidence that 1080 affected avian testicular development. Notwithstanding this preliminary data, however, the Agency noted its continued concerns regarding the possible reproductive effects of 1080 on the condor.

b. Comments

The CDFA devoted much of its comment on PD 2/3 to the Agency's analysis of risk to the condor. In addition to specific comments on Agency interpretation of data, CDFA made some general comments about the condor and its plight that are discussed below. This is followed by an analysis of more specific comments on data interpretation, risk analysis, etc. CDFA contended, among other things that:

    i. The condor was on its way to extinction long before California was settled by Europeans.

    ii. There is no evidence that there was an upsurge in mortality among condors following the first few years of use of 1080.

   iii. There is no evidence that 1080 has been responsible for a single condor death.

    iv. No hard evidence or subjective evidence was found to support any mortality to condors from 1080 used for field rodent control.

    v. There is no convincing subjective or hard evidence to support the theory that 1080 may be implicated in the reproductive failure of condors.

CDFA offered several comments concerning the use of the turkey vulture as a surrogate species for the condor. They noted that:

    i. The turkey vulture is the closest representative to the condor and is a reasonable surrogate.

    ii. There is no substantiated evidence that 1080 has been responsible for the death of turkey vultures (Hegdal et al. 1979).

   iii. Turkey vultures, which feed on 1080 poisoned ground squirrels, are as plentiful today in California as they have ever been after 35 years of 1080 use.

CDFA offered several comments on the Agency's discussion of condor feeding habits and in particular commented that information referenced by EPA in PD 2/3 establishes that ground squirrels represent only a small part of the condor's diet. Thus, CDFA argued that any ground squirrels consumed by a condor would be diluted with other foods in its diet, which makes the risk to the condor much less than the Agency contended.

CDFA commented that the Agency failed to account for the tendency of turkey vultures and condors to regurgitate food, that this characteristic is common in many avian scavengers and is probably the mechanism by which they protect themselves from a variety of toxic substances.

CDFA also objected to the importance the Agency placed on the fact that ground squirrels will carry grain in their cheek pouches and this could lead to a high concentration of 1080 treated bait that may be ingested by a condor. Based on its considerable field experience and expertise, CDFA made several points regarding pouching. They are:

i. Pouching is rarely done by young squirrels, which make up the bulk (80%) of the ground squirrel population at the time of the year when most baiting is done.

ii. Even when pouching is occurring, it may not mean that a high percentage of squirrels have pouched 1080 bait.

iii. When some squirrels began to feel sick they will empty their cheek pouches.

iv. Some ground squirrel species only rarely have anything in their pouches.

v. It is not uncommon for a scavenger to remove the skin from the skull, thus scattering any bait which may be in the pouches.

CDFA further argued that there is very little risk to condors based on the failure to find any condor dying from 1080 poisoning. Specifically, CDFA took issue with the Agency's contention that 1080 is a slow acting poison and therefore if a condor were poisoned it would likely succomb in an area remote from the control operation and probably not be found. CDFA also cites that time spent by condors at a feeding site is an important factor in determining whether or not a dead condor might be found. They also note that most of the condor nesting, roosting and feeding areas are well known and monitored by those working with condors making the likelihood that a dead condor would go unnoticed small.

c. Agency Response

While the Agency generally does not disagree with CDFA's overview comments about the condor, the report by Hagen (1972) that a condor killed by flying into a transmission line contained 1080 in its digestive tract is still of concern. Sublethal effects in birds often include ataxia, a loss of coordination of voluntary muscle movements. As pointed out in PD 2/3 there was no way to conclude that the 1080 did not impair the condor's faculties or any indication how the condor came in contact with the 1080. CDFA offered no specific comment on the Hagen report.

Notwithstanding general agreement about the lack of evidence implicating 1080 in the death of any condor, the Agency's concern is focused on the fact that the condor is in critical danger of becoming extinct and condors are exposed to 1080 by feeding on poisoned ground squirrels. The Agency's position and responsibility is to ensure that the use of 1080 for rodent control does not result in additional pressure on the condor's ability to survive. Therefore, all available data have been evaluated from a conservative margin of safety perspective.

The Agency agrees with CDFA's assessment regarding the turkey vulture, but believes its use as a surrogate species for the endangered condor has certain limitations. The Agency will not accept LD50 values for the turkey or black vulture as an approximate LD50 for the condor.

The Agency noted in PD 2/3 that while turkey vultures and condors are both carrion feeders and belong to the same family, they are of different genera and as such their susceptability to 1080 may or may not be similar. There is no way to predict the susceptability of a particular species to 1080. Therefore, the Agency believes that in order to provide the greatest degree of protection for this species, the toxicity of the most sensitive avian species should be considered in determining a regulatory position.

Regarding CDFA's comments on condor feeding habits, the Agency recognizes that the condor does not limit its feeding to ground squirrels, but there is evidence that condors commonly feed on them. In addition, in the absence of specific information, EPA assumes that condors will feed on stomachs and cheek pouches of ground squirrels, though not necessarily selectively. The Agency is particularly concerned about those situations where ground squirrel carcasses are plentiful and other food sources are scarce. This scenario could lead to feeding episodes where poisoned ground squirrels constitute all or most of a condor's diet.

The Agency agrees with CDFA that the ability to regurgitate may be an important factor in self protection for the condor, but, as CDFA also noted, this factor alone may or may not be enough of a safety factor to save an exposed individual; coyotes may also regurgitate poisons, yet they are susceptable to 1080.

The points raised by CDFA on pouching habits of ground squirrels do not significantly diminish the Agency's concern, described in PD 2/3, concerning the potential for a condor to feed on squirrels that might contain large amounts of treated bait in their pouches.

The Agency does not disagree with the observations and comments of CDFA regarding the time spent by condors at feeding sites, or the high level of monitoring and tracking devoted to individual condors. The Agency is persuaded that the high level of observation and interest in the condor by various groups may make the likelihood of a dead condor going undetected less than the Agency originally speculated. California, however, did not support its contention with any estimates of what fraction of condors that have died in recent years were, in fact, found.

In summary, CDFA has raised many valid points concerning condor feeding habits, characteristics, exposure, and lack of evidence attributing any condor death to 1080. However, the Agency believes that the comments presented by CDFA do not eliminate the risk potential to the condor identified by the Agency in PD 2/3. The Agency must ensure that the use of 1080 as a field rodenticide does not impose an increased burden on the condor's ability to survive. The Agency views the loss of a single condor to 1080 as a threat to the survival of the species. This position necessitates a conservative evaluation of data such as LD50's, that considers not only biologically closely related species but the most sensitive avian species. It also necessitates consideration of feeding and exposure situations that may not be likely to occur, but are still possible under certain conditions and must be considered.

The Agency has proposed continued use of 1080 in the range of the condor, but at reduced bait concentration levels. However, a recent biological opinion from the Office of Endangered Species (OES) that use of the 1080 livestock protection collar would jeopardize the continued existence of the condor necessitates further discussion with OES on the use of 1080 baits in the condor's range. The Agency considers the condor's range to be that as defined by OES in their biological opinion on the livestock collar. It includes the California counties of Fresno, Kern, King, Los Angeles, Monterey, San Benito, San Luis Obispo, Santa Barbara, Tulare, and Ventura.

It is possible that 1080 baits will be prohibited in the range of the California condor until safety data are submitted and evaluated.

The Agency believes the regulatory decision contained in Chapter V of this document reflects consideration of the field and regulatory expertise of CDFA, the California Department of Fish and Game, and the County Agricultural Commissioners' Offices.

2. San Joaquin Kit Fox

a. Agency Position in PD 2/3

In PD 2/3 the Agency noted that while there were no confirmed reports of kit foxes being killed from 1080 used in ground squirrel control programs, the potential for adverse effects was very high considering the approximate 1080 LD 50 value for the kit fox of 0.22 mg/kg. The Agency noted that this degree of sensitivity approached that of the coyote, which is approximately 0.1 mg/kg, and Heqdal (1979) clearly demonstrated that 1080 ground squirrel control programs resulted in substantial coyote mortality.

b. Comments

CDFA offered several comments on the Agency's assessment of risk to the San Joaquin kit fox.

In PD 2/3 the Agency cited reports by researchers that indicated that:

i. San Joaquin kit foxes will eat ground squirrel carrion (Laughrin 1970; Morrell 1971, 1972).

ii. 1080 rodent control programs may kill some kit foxes, but do not threaten the population (Swick 1973, Morrell 1975).

iii. Field evaluations have indicated that ground squirrels frequently consume several lethal doses of 1080 before death (Swick 1973).

On point i, CDFA commented that kit fox prey almost entirely on live kangaroo rats, pocket mice, San Joaquin antelope ground squirrel, and probably as carrion, two species of rabbit and minimally the California ground squirrel.

On point ii, CDFA noted that the quote attributed to Swick, concerning statements from the San Luis Obispo County Agriculture Department regarding kit fox losses in rodent control programs, could not be verified.

On point iii, CDFA questioned EPA's characterization of the amounts of 1080 found in ground squirrels as "several lethal doses."

CDFA noted that none of the authors discussed above came up with evidence that a single kit fox was ever killed by 1080 and that no other kit fox fatalities have been attributed to 1080

CDFA objected to the Agency citing the 1975 Schitosky study involving one desert kit fox as evidence for the RPAR criteria for endangered species being met. CDFA noted that the test, which involved gavaging a kangaroo rat with a massive dose of 1080 and then feeding it to the kit fox, in no way ressembles what occurs in the field.

CDFA noted that according to Morrell (1975) the estimated kit fox population was a minimum of 5,066 and a maximum of 14,800 adults with a mean figure of 10,000. In another section of their response they state that these figures represent the current kit fox population. CDFA cites Dana (1976) that there were believed to be only 1,000-3,000 kit foxes when they were placed on the endangered list in 1967. They also point out that the kit fox recovery team recommended recently that the kit fox status be downgraded from endangered to threatened.

CDFA speculated that alternative rodenticides may be less efficacious and present more of a hazard to nontarget animals, particularly birds, including condors. They cite Schitosky (1975), who contends that zinc phosphide is the safest to kit foxes among three rodenticides tested (including strychnine and 1080) but its use results in a greater percentage of squirrels dying above ground rather than in their burrows. This presumably would increase the risk to condors and other birds.

CDFA also speculated that resident foxes in ground squirrel control areas may have developed an aversion to 1080 killed ground squirrels and/or developed a tolerance through ingestion and emesis of sublethal doses.

Defenders of Wildlife commented that the use of 1080 is inappropriate in the range of the kit fox, even when one-mile buffer zones around active dens are excluded from treatment.

c. Agency Response

Regarding CDFA's comment on the minimal role ground squirrels play in the kit fox diet, the Agency agrees that the California ground squirrel may indeed make up a small or even insignificant portion of the diet. However, as with the condor, the Agency is concerned about unusual circumstances, when "normal" or preferred food is not available or is scarce. In these instances the California ground squirrel carcasses could become a large part of the kit fox's diet on an interim basis.

The Agency has no reason to doubt the accuracy of the Swick comment and notes that the observation may have been made by an employee no longer with the county. In any event, it underscores the Agency's concern that the potential for poisoning of kit foxes does exist.

Regarding CDFA's questions about ground squirrel consumption of "several lethal doses" of 1080, the Agency notes that the size of the lethal dose in relation to the amount consumed is important for some purposes. CDFA does not dispute that data show that dead ground squirrels have been recovered and analyzed and shown to contain significant quantities of unmetabolized 1080. Moreover, it is not in dispute that kit foxes could ingest such 1080 by eating the ground squirrels. Although CDFA is correct that the Agency does not report the LD100 for the California ground squirrel it does report the LD50, a value which is appropriate for making calculations of potential hazard. The focus of Agency concern in this regard is that the poisoning action of 1080 is such that it may allow, in some cases, time for squirrels to consume more bait than needed to cause death. This fact heightens the concern about the amount of 1080 a kit fox might be exposed to from feeding on a 1080 killed ground squirrel. Further, as expressed in PD 2/3, the Agency is concerned with the loss of a single kit fox, although the level of concern is less than for the condor.

The Agency acknowledges that there is no hard evidence that any kit fox has been killed with 1080, however there are convincing facts such as the feeding habits of the kit fox, LD 50 values of surrogate species and the California ground squirrel, that indicate the potential for kit fox loss from 1080 baiting programs. Additionally, Spencer (1945) reported kit fox mortality associated with ground squirrel baiting with 1080, although no confirmatory chemical analysis was conducted.

The Agency agrees that the Schitosky study was not conducted in such a manner to allow any definitive conclusions about the fate of a kit fox feeding on 1080 killed rodents.

The Agency has the following response concerning CDFA's comments on the estimated kit fox population and its current endangered status. The San Joaquin Kit Fox Recovery Plan published by the U.S. Fish and Wildlife Service, January 31, 1983, does note that the 1969 population was estimated at between 1,000 and 3,000 animals. The Recovery Plan also notes that the Morrell study of 1975 was a more thorough quantitative study than earlier ones, but that the population estimate of 14,832 was of doubtful value since no correction was made for the loss of suitable habitat. The Recovery Plan presents adjusted figures based on the Morrell study of a maximum population of 6,961. The Plan also notes that the Morrell data must be interpreted with caution because only 1 percent of the total range was surveyed. The Plan estimates the San Joaquin kit fox population prior to 1930 may have been between 8,667 and 12,134 based on densities of 1 to 1.4 foxes per square mile and a range of 8,667 square miles. It is further noted that the 1975 adjusted population estimate of 6,961 represents a possible population decline of 20-43% in the last half century.

The Recovery Plan does not present a definitive picture of the population at the time the kit fox was listed nor the current population although it appears that it has stabilized. The Plan does not support the implication of CDFA's comment that the kit fox population has increased since endangered species listing. Further, no mention of downgrading the status of the kit fox was noted by the Agency in its review of the Recovery Plan. The San Joaquin kit fox is still listed as an edangered species by OES.

Regarding CDFA's comments about the use of zinc phosphide resulting in more ground squirrel deaths above ground, the Agency notes that the mode of poisoning action with zinc phosphide does not generally result in secondary poisoning concerns. When ingested, zinc phosphide generates phosphene gas, which normally renders the carcasses relatively harmless as the gas is quickly dissipated. The Agency is also of course concerned with the question raised by CDFA regarding the use of less efficacious rodenticides that result in more baiting. This includes concern over lowering the concentration of a pesticide to a level that is ineffective.

The Agency acknowledges that CDFA's hypothesis about aversive conditioning and 1080 tolerance build up in the kit fox is possible, but there are no specific data on this phenomena.

The Agency believes the 1 mile buffer zone from any kit fox den that is now required by California, in addition to the other stringent regulatory controls imposed by California on 1080 use, as well as the modifications in the terms and conditions of use required by this document will provide added protection for the kit fox until more definitive data become available.

3. Black-footed ferret

a. Agency Position in PD 2/3

The Agency concluded that there was no "margin of safety" for the black-footed ferret from the use of 1080 to control prairie dogs. This conclusion was based on the LD 50 values of the prairie dog, the amount of 1080 treated bait that a prairie dog might consume, assumptions about the amount of 1080 that might not be metabolized following ingestion of bait by the prairie dog, and LD 50 values of species related to the black-footed ferret.

Specifically, the Agency suggested that if a one kg prairie dog consumed as little as 4 grams of a .11% bait (the concentration of the only bait available for prairie dog control), 4.4 mg of 1080 would be ingested. The Agency went on to note that only 0.3 mg of absorbed 1080 may be sufficient to kill a prairie dog based on existing LD 50 values and therefore much of the 1080 consumed by a prairie dog would not be detoxified.

b. Comments

CDFA commented that the Agency's attempt to show no margin of safety for the ferret was not very convincing. They contended that if 75 percent of the 1080 consumed was detoxified, a rate of detoxification suggested by the Agency in PD 2/3, only 1.1 mg of 1080 would remain in the carcass of a prairie dog, using the example cited by the Agency in part (a) of this section. They further speculated that if the black-footed ferret is equally susceptible to 1080 as the domestic ferret (LD50 of 1.41 mg/kg) then a LD 50 would still not be reached if a one kg black-footed ferret consumed the entire prairie dog containing 1.1 mg. CDFA also commented that a one kg ferret would not consume more than 10 percent of its weight or in this case 100 grams of food a day. Their conclusion was that there is apparently little if any risk to the black-footed ferret.

c. Agency Response

The Agency is not persuaded by CDFA's analysis that little or no risk exists. The Agency cannot unduly rely on the 75% detoxification factor, which has been calculated from a single small test. As noted in several discussions in this document, the wide variability in toxicological response of related species to 1080 is of concern to the Agency and it cannot base its calculations solely on one surrogate species. In this regard, the Agency also notes that another species of the same genus, the mink ($\underline{M}$. $\underline{vison}$), has LD 50 values reported between $0.49 - 1$ mg/kg, which is less than the reported LD 50 value for the domestic ferret (1.41 mg/kg-more recent data show an LD_{50} of 1.23 mg/kg). Therefore, the Agency believes that it may be reasonably extrapolated from available data that the use of 1080 may pose risk to black-footed ferrets.

4. Aleutian Canada goose

a. Agency Position in PD 2/3

In PD 2/3 the Agency indicated that USDI had concluded that the use of 1080 under current label conditions was not likely to jeopardize the continued existence of the Aleutian Canada goose. EPA believed that a greater degree of concern was warranted because 1080 is used to control ground squirrels on the dikes of rice fields, an area where geese may feed when the fields are fallow. The Agency also noted that while the geese may feed primarily on herbaceous matter, there was concern that they may also feed on treated grain bait when available.

b. Comments

CDFA recommended that USDI's determination be relied upon and expressed concern that alternative rodenticides may result in geese fatalities.

c. Agency response

The Agency has considered the points raised by CDFA and concludes that the risks to the Aleutian Canada goose can be significantly reduced when 1080 is used in accordance with the CDFA program recently approved for strychnine and other toxicants.

III. Comments and Agency Response on the Position
   Document 2/3 Benefits Analysis

   A. Agency Position in PD 2/3

        In the PD 2/3, the Agency evaluated the economic
impacts of denying registration of 1080 for federal and
intrastate registered rodenticidal uses. The general approach
of that economic analysis was to evaluate the economic impacts
assuming 1080 was cancelled and users shift to alternative
materials or systems. The analysis identified or estimated
the quantity of registered 1080 bait used, listed registered
alternatives, and determined changes in treatment costs
associated with the use of the most likely alternative rodent
control methods.

        Compound 1080 is primarily used to control ground squirrels,
prairie dogs, and field rodents. It is perceived that control
of ground squirrels and prairie dogs is necessary because these
rodents compete with cattle for grass and leave holes in the
ground which domisticated animals can step in or which are
sources of erosion. The field rodents eat grain.

        The Agency's conclusions regarding economic effects were
based on information from a number of sources, principally the
Preliminary Benefit Analysis. In addition, rebuttal comments
from registrants, users, USDA and other parties, federal and
state vertebrate pest control specialists and available
published data were considered in the Agency's conclusions.

        The Preliminary Benefit Analysis focused on agricultural
uses (pastures and croplands) to control rodent pests in forage,
and nonagricultural uses primarily for the control of commensal
rodents. Within these two categories, the Agency identified
major and minor uses to the extent that data permitted, estimated
quantities of 1080 used and listed available alternatives
including an evaluation of their efficacy and availability.

        The Agency faced considerable data limitations in performing
the economic analysis of denying 1080 uses. In most cases,
data necessary for accurately determining economic effects
were lacking. For example, almost no field test data were found
regarding the comparative efficacy of 1080 and alternatives
under the complex set of climatic, topographic and soil
conditions on a site-by-site, species-by-species basis.
Likewise, few statistically valid field surveys or data were
found on the extent of pest infestation and the damage caused
by various rodent species on individual sites. As a result
of these data limitations, the Agency relied on the judgement
of knowledgeable Federal, state and local vertebrate pest control specialists in the evaluation of economic consequences
of denying uses of 1080. Thus, this analysis often resulted
in qualitative discussions of impacts rather than quantitative
estimates.

In summary the Agency concluded that 1080 was the most efficacious and cost effective single dose rodenticide available for control of field and commensal rodents. Treatment costs with strychnine and zinc phosphide, the principal alternatives to 1080, increased costs an estimated 60 to 80% for the control of ground squirrels and prairie dogs. These increased costs resulted from both higher bait costs and the need in many instances to prebait. The Agency concluded that chemical controls (including strychnine and zinc phosphide) and non-chemical controls can be effective when properly used, however, they were usually more labor intensive, more costly and generally thought to be less effective than 1080.

The Agency concluded that local impacts on agricultural productivity or production costs could occur in Colorado, Oregon, and California, where there are active 1080 use programs, but that the economic impact of denying all uses of 1080 would not seriously affect U.S. production or prices of major commodites or services.

B. Comments on PD 2/3

No significant, supported, new benefit information was submitted in response to the PD 2/3. USDA, California, Montana, Nevada, South Dakota, Wyoming, several farm and ranch organizations, as well as individual farmers commented on various aspects of the benefits discussion presented in PD 2/3.

USDA expressed concern that the Agency's action would lead to the unavailability of efficacious, cost effective, and safe tools for the control of field rodents. They recommended that the Agency delay any final decision on 1080 until the results of several ongoing cooperative studies were completed. USDA maintained that these studies would provide critical information on environmental impacts and costs.

CDFA commented that if 1080 were not available, annual losses of $2 billion would be incurred eventually. California based farm and ranch organizations also cited the $2 billion figure, but neither CDFA or any organization submitted documentation to support this estimate.

Montana expressed concern that the use and benefits information they had gathered during the use of 1080 on an emergency basis under §18 of FIFRA for control of Columbian ground squirrels was not included in PD 2/3 and should be included in the Agency's decision.

Nevada commented that 1080 may be preferable in some situations to available rodenticides and recommended that certain uses proposed by the Agency for denial be kept.

The South Dakota Department of Agriculture (South Dakota) made two comments that related directly to the benefit analysis. First they commented that the Agency had not sufficiently addressed the "testimony of field rodent control professionals that the zinc phosphide yields inconsistent results for prairie dog control." The second comment concerned the adverse economic impact suffered by South Dakota agricultural producers because of the unavailability of 1080 for prairie dog control in their state. South Dakota estimated that the cost of zinc phosphide was $784,000 greater that the cost of treating the same acreage with 1080.

Wyoming claimed that state agricultural production would be severely impacted if 1080 were not made available.

Several other commenters, mostly ranchers and farmers, stated that there was a need for field rodent control, and that 1080 was an efficacious and viable chemical.

C. Agency Response

The future availability of 1080 will now depend upon the willingness of registrants and other interested parties to develop the data necessary to support Federal registration. While data are being generated the Agency has decided to allow the continued use of 1080 for all rodent species and sites contained on current labels with certain modifications, with the possible exception in the range of the California condor. The Agency notes that USDA's comments about ongoing studies were made in November, 1983 but, to date, the results of these studies have not been submitted to the Agency.

In the absence of supporting data, the Agency cannot utilize the $2 billion agricultural impact estimate reported by CDFA and other California agricultural organizations. The Agency does note that it would appear that a chemical of that much economic importance would be readily supported with data necessary for Federal registration.

The Agency did not consider the benefits and use information from the Montana Columbian ground squirrel programs in developing PD 2/3 because the Agency only addressed Federally registered or intrastate products. As noted earlier the Columbian ground squirrel use was permitted under the emergency exemption provisions of § 18 of FIFRA. This provision permits use only in unusual or emergency circumstances. However, the benefits information submitted by Montana has been reviewed in the preparation of this position document. The Agency concluded that the Columbian ground squirrel information cannot be extrapolated to other field rodent uses and does not alter the Agency's benefit assessment in PD 2/3. The information gathered by Montana will be useful in supporting a Federal registration for Columbian ground squirrel control.

Nevada did not provide any quantitative benefits information necessary for the Agency to assess the economic impact of their suggestion.

In response to South Dakota's comments the Agency notes that it reviewed all pertinent data, gathered information from zinc phosphide prairie dog control programs conducted in South Dakota and elsewhere, and collected information from local state, and Federal vertebrate pest control specialists in assessing the efficacy of zinc phosphide. The Agency believes its efficacy assessment of zinc phosphide presented in PD 2/3 is correct.

On South Dakota's second comment, the Agency notes that it did not specifically address the impact on benefits in states that did not have intrastate registrations, which would include South Dakota. The Agency did note in PD 2/3 that areas that did not have 1080 available were at a comparative disadvantage where alternatives were more costly or not as effective. The Agency has some questions about the dollar amount presented by South Dakota in that it was assumed that the entire acreage of prairie dog inhabited lands was treated. In addition the $784,000 is small compared to the total estimated value of cattle, calf, and sheep production in the State ($1.4 billion in 1982). As detailed in Section IV, the Agency intends to allow the continued use of 1080 for prairie dog control under certain strict conditions. South Dakota, however, will have to obtain a §3 Federal registration prior to the use of 1080 in South Dakota for prairie dogs or other rodents, as will all states that do not have a current intra-state registration for 1080.

The Agency could not evaluate the statements of Wyoming and the several ranchers and farmers who commented on the agricultural impact of not being able to use 1080, because no supporting data were submitted.

The Agency also notes with interest the development of certain benefits information associated with the use of 1080 to control prairie dogs. The high potential risks to the endangered black-footed ferret from the use of chemical controls has resulted in questions being raised about the ultimate benefits of chemical control programs. Certain new information, which is discussed briefly in section D of this chapter, indicates that improved range management and cultural practices may be viable alternatives to toxicants under certain conditions. Although this information relates directly to prairie dog control, the principals may be applicable to the control of ground squirrels and other rodents as well.

D. <u>New Information</u>

Recent studies with the management of lands containing
large prairie dog populations suggest that cultural control
may be a viable alternative to the use of 1080 or other
toxicants in some circumstances. Prairie dog towns are
generally associated with range areas which are heavily
grazed by cattle. It appears that prairie dogs rely on the
cattle to keep the grass in and around the prairie dog town
short. If the cattle are removed, the prairie dogs are
not always able to keep the grass short. Tall grass provides
cover for animals which prey on prairie dogs, such as coyotes.
As the grass cover increases, the efficiency of the predators
increases to the point that the prairie dog population begins
to decline. Snell (1984) describes a successful program in
which a 110 acre prairie dog town was reduced to less than 10
acres by reducing grazing of the prairie dog town by cattle.
This method may reduce the need for broad scale poisoning of
prairie dogs, especially where it is practical to control the
level of cattle grazing or where overgrazing has contributed
to the prairie dog infestation.

IV. Comments and Agency Response on Proposed Regulatory
    Actions in Position Document 2/3

    This chapter summarizes the Agency's proposed actions in
PD 2/3 for each use, presents the comments on these proposals,
and the Agency's response to the comments.

A. Rangeland, Cropland, and Non-Agricultural Sites: Ground
   Squirrels

    1. Proposed Actions in PD 2/3

    In PD 2/3, the Agency proposed several modifications
in the terms and conditions of use. Most of these modifications
were to be incorporated on product labels.

    a. Standardize bait concentrations at a maximum of 0.02
percent active ingredient and application rate of one level
teaspoon per burrow for hand application, a maximum of 0.02%
active ingredient and application rate of four pounds per acre
for broadcast application of grain bait, and a maximum of 0.02%
active ingredient and a application rate of five to ten pounds
per acre for broadcast application of green bait.

    b. Standardize hand baiting and post-baiting procedures
as follows:

        i. Baiting should not be done unless tests indicate
           satisfactory bait acceptance will occur in areas
           to be treated.
       ii. Keep pets and domestic animals away from treated
           areas.
      iii. Clean up all accidentally spilled bait immediately.
       iv. Do not place bait in piles.
        v. Pick up and burn or bury deeply all visible carcass
           of animals killed by 1080.
       vi. Do not use within 1/4 mile of a dwelling without
           first notifying the occupants.
      vii. All bait must be dyed yellow in accordance with the
           California Vertebrate Pest Control Handbook.

    c. Standardize aerial baiting and post-baiting procedure
as follows:

        i. Use in accordance with the Guidelines for Applying
           Rodent Baits by Aircraft for Control of Ground
           Squirrels in the California Vertebrate Pest Control
           Handbook.
       ii. Pick up and burn or bury deeply all visible carcasses
           of animals killed by 1080.
      iii. All bait must be dyed yellow in accordance with the
           California Vertebrate Pest Control Handbook.

d. To protect the California condor, the following requirement was proposed:

> Do not use in the Sespe-Sierra range of the California condor or in that portion of the coastal range south of Monterey County. Do not use in the coastal range north of San Luis Obispo County during the months of August through December.

e. To protect the San Joaquin kit fox, the following requirements were proposed:

> Do not use in that portion of the range of the San Joaquin kit fox that has been closed to night hunting by the California Fish and Game Commission. In the remainder of the range, consult the California Fish and Game Commission prior to use.

f. To protect the Morro Bay kangaroo rat, the following requirement was proposed:

> Do not use in the range of the Morro Bay kangaroo rat, as defined by the United States Fish and Wildlife Service.

g. To protect the salt marsh harvest mouse, the following requirement was proposed:

> Do not use in the range of the salt marsh harvest mouse, as defined by the United States Fish and Wildlife Service.

h. To protect the Aleutian Canada goose the following requirements were proposed:

> Do not use from September 1 to April 30 for the control of ground squirrels on croplands within the areas closed by the California Department of Fish and Game to the hunting of Canada Geese. Additionally, any baiting for ground squirrels in the wetlands areas of Contra Costa, San Joaquin, Solana and Yolo Counties from September 1 to April 30 is permitted only if bait stations are use in accordance with the California Vertebrate Control Handbook.

2. Comments on PD 2/3

Many commenters responded to these proposals. On the proposal to reduce and standardize 1080 bait concentrations at .02%, commenters (Montana, CDFA, Colorado Department of Agriculture, New Mexico Department of Agriculture and USDA) expressed concern that the proposed bait concentrations

had not been shown to be or would not be efficacious. USDA
commented that any reduction of active ingredient not based
on efficacy data may significantly reduce efficacy, thus
rendering the bait ineffective for achieving control, while
increasing costs because of the subsequent need for multiple
applications. This could potentially increase the hazard to
nontarget species. USDA also cited work by Salmon and
Lickliter (1982) that showed that standard bait concentrations
could not be applied across species. USDA pointed out
that if the target animal does not ingest enough bait to
cause death, not only is control ineffective but future
control may also become more difficult because of bait shyness.

USDA recommended that any reduction and standardization
of bait concentration and application rate be based on scientific
studies and that the proposal in PD 2/3 be delayed until data
are developed to determine the field efficacy of various
dosage rates. USDA noted that such studies could be done
rapidly at reasonable cost.

The California Farm Bureau Federation characterized the
proposed bait reduction requirement as unacceptable and noted
that California officials had already reduced the bait concentration
to those levels that retained the necessary effectiveness. They
also cited the State's extensive experience with 1080 as a reason
for retaining the current range of bait concentrations. The
California Cattleman's Association echoed the Farm Bureau's
sentiment regarding the State's experience with 1080. They also
expressed concern that lowering bait concentrations to levels
that would make baits ineffective would force excessive repeated
use and would result in less effective control and more toxic
bait in the environment.

On proposals to standardize hand and aerial baiting and
post-baiting procedures, commenters (USDA, Montana, and
California) pointed out that some of these measures (keeping
pets away, and burning or burying visible carcasses) were not
always possible. Specifically, USDA noted that it was not
practical under range conditions to pick up and burn carcasses
because of the risk of plague or parasite infestations to
those humans responsible for disposal. They also noted that
soil conditions may prohibit burying and fire hazards prohibit
the burning of carcasses. Montana noted that it was impractical
and unrealistic to pick up and burn or bury carcasses on large
or inaccessable baited areas. Montana recommended that carcasses
be buried singularly, in order to lessen the risk from a
concentration of carcasses, that could be dug up by scavengers.
Commenters also noted that dye colors for baits should be
allowed to vary depending on local conditions and the California
Vertebrate Pest Control Handbook has legal force only in
California.

On the proposal to impose geographic restrictions to protect the California condor, commenters (CDFA and USDA) said that the geographic range restrictions were not justified in light of California's efforts to protect this endangered species. USDA agreed that since the risk to condors was small and theoretical in nature, the Agency should permit the use of 1080 for ground squirrel control in the range of the condor consistent with current California policy. California's policy is that a label must specify when a pesticide is to be used in defined endangered species areas. They further noted that the Agency's final position on strychnine used for ground squirrel control in the range of the condor was consistent with California's policy. CDFA offered extensive comments on the Agency's risk analysis to the condor which were discussed in Section II of this document.

On the proposal concerning geographic restrictions for the protection of the San Joaquin kit fox, USDA stated that EPA had chosen to ignore the data of Swick (1973) and Morrell (1975) and had instead relied on assumptions based on LD 50's and studies on another species, the coyote. They further noted that the Agency admits that they were unaware of reports verifying that kit foxes had been killed by 1080. USDA recommended that EPA concur with California policy and regulation for protection of the San Joaquin kit fox. CDFA also presented numerous comments on the Agency's risk analysis to the kit fox. These comments were addressed in Section II of this document.

On the proposal to establish geographic restrictions to protect the Morro Bay kangaroo rat and the salt marsh harvest mouse respectively, USDA objected to the Agency proposal to prohibit use in the range of these species and notes that PD 2/3 does not provide scientific justification for these actions nor a discussion of the potential impact such action would have.

On the proposal to place seasonal restrictions on 1080 baiting to protect the Aleutian Canada goose, CDFA commented on the lack of demonstrated risk to the goose and the fact that EPA ignored the advice of USDI. They also noted that they would concur with restrictions for the goose if they were in accord with the recommendations of California governmental agencies. These comments were discussed in Section II of this document.

3. Agency Response

Concerning proposal (a), reduction and standardization of bait concentration and application rate, the Agency agrees that any reduction to levels that are ineffective could have adverse consequences. The Agency also agrees that the soundest way to determine the optimum bait concentration and application rate is with valid test data. The Agency also agrees with USDA's comment that such tests could be performed quickly and at reasonable cost. However, no data have been generated or even initiated in the several years since the beginning of the Special Review or in the last year since the issuance of PD 2/3. The Agency has modified its position to permit use at current bait concentrations and application rates until data for registration are generated except in the range of the condor. However, as discussed more fully in Chapter V, a recent biological opinion submitted to the Agency from USDI's Office of Endangered Species (OES) on the use of the 1080 livestock protection collar necessitates further evaluation of the use of 1080 baits in the range of the condor. OES stated that the use of the collar would jeopardize the continued existence of the condor. Use in 1985 baiting programs will be allowed under current label requirements. If permitted, beginning in 1986, the use of 1080 in the range of the condor will be at a maximum bait concentration of .02% until field efficacy data are generated. If the .02% level is not effective, the level will be changed when data establishing the lowest effective bait concentration are submitted as well as data showing that this level will not impact on the condor.

Concerning the standardization of hand baiting and post-baiting procedures, the Agency agrees that the requirement to keep pets and domestic animals away is overly restrictive, and would, as a practical matter, prohibit use since there are very few places where free-roaming pets and livestock do not occasionally occur. The requirement has been revised. The Agency also agrees that the proposed requirement to bury or burn all visible carcasses cannot be reasonably implemented in some situations and has revised this requirement.

The Agency disagrees that its proposal to require dyeing of rodenticide baits as specified in the California Vertebrate Pest Control Handbook is too restrictive and warrants modification. One of California's purposes in dyeing 1080 grain baits is to protect seed eating birds. Field trials with Auramine O, a yellow dye, showed limited impacts on avain species, which may have been due to repellency caused by the dye. Therefore, the Agency is requiring that all 1080 grain baits used for field rodent control be dyed yellow.

The Agency has modified its position concerning the imposition of certain geographic and seasonal use restrictions to protect the endangered California condor, San Joaquin kit fox, Morro Bay kangaroo rat, salt marsh harvest mouse and the Aleutian Canada goose.

The Agency proposed these restrictions to provide adequate protection for the identified endangered species. However, it is the Agency's belief that in this instance the development and administration of programs to protect most endangered species will be most effectively carried out at the state and local level. All the endangered species identified in the preceeding paragraph are potentially exposed to 1080 rodent baits only in California. Based on comments and documents submitted by various State Agencies in California responsible for pesticide regulation and fish and wildlife management, the Agency is now convinced that the best interests of endangered species protection will be served by withdrawing the proposed geographical and seasonal restrictions for all species. The Agency believes that certain measures instituted in California are of particular importance in protecting endangered species. These measures include:

  ° The stringent regulatory controls imposed by California officials on the use and possession of 1080.

  ° The Joint Policy Statement regarding rare and endangered species signed by CDFA, the California Department of Fish and Game, and the California Agricultural Commissioners Association.

  ° The considerable field experience and training of state employees involved with the distribution and use of 1080.

The Agency will require that specific programs developed for endangered species by California officials be submitted to the Agency for review and approval prior to 1080 use in the range of the California condor and kit fox. Existing programs for the salt marsh harvest mouse, Morro Bay kangaroo rat and Aleutian Canada goose are now acceptable. Any subsequent program changes must also be submitted to EPA for review. As part of EPA's review the Office of Endangered Species, USDI, will be consulted. Specific label instructions and cautions regarding endangered species will be required. These label statements are detailed in Chapter V.

B. Rangeland and Cropland: Prairie Dogs

1. Proposed Actions in PD 2/3

In PD 2/3, the Agency proposed the following modifications of the terms and conditions of registration for this use:

a. Standardize bait concentration at a maximum of 0.02% active ingredient at a dosage of one teaspoon per burrow spread over a three square feet area.

b. Standardize baiting and post-baiting procedures in the same manner as proposed for "Rangeland and Cropland Rodents: Ground Squirrels."

c. Restrict use to governmental agencies or persons under the direct supervision of members of governmental agencies.

d. Allow the use of 1080 in a prairie dog town only if a precontrol survey, conducted in accordance with a protocol approved by EPA, in consultation with USFWS, does not indicate the presence or possible presence of a blackfooted ferret.

2. Comments

USDA, and several state and county agencies responded to the above proposals. Concerning proposal (a), reduction in bait concentration and application rate, USDA quoted from PD 2/3 that "The Agency has no direct data to specify an active ingredient concentration of less than 0.11 percent." USDA, therefore, recommended that the bait concentration of 1080 for prairie dog control remain the same until studies by the Fish and Wildlife Service are completed. New Mexico also took issue with the Agency's proposal and noted the inadequacy of basing the bait reduction on LD 50 values rather than field efficacy data. South Dakota made similar observations stating that the only realistic way to determine the lowest concentration level is by actually testing the bait under conditions encountered in the field. Montana commented that time and money are needed to insure adequate field testing of the 0.02% bait and if it is efficacious it should be made available to all states. Colorado, which has the only permissible product for prairie dog control, commented that based on their many years of field experience the 0.02% bait concentration level and application rate of 1 teaspoonful per burrow would not work. Colorado also questioned where the Agency's supporting data are for justifying the 0.02% level. The Board of County Commissioners in Ouray and Bent County, Colorado, also expressed concern that lowering the bait concentration would result in reduced efficacy and the need for additional baiting.

Concerning proposal (b), standardization of baiting and post-baiting procedures, USDA commented that the same objections that applied to ground squirrels apply to prairie dogs. They also noted that the hazard with prairie dogs appears to be with the black-footed ferret and few if any ferrets are known to exist in Colorado.

USDA and New Mexico commented that proposal (c), limitation of use to government agencies or persons under the direct supervision of members of government agencies, was unnecessary and not justified. Both recommended that use be allowed by certified applicators. USDA noted that no government agency has a sufficient number of trained people to carry out a large program without assistance of the private landowner and that such a requirement would add significant additional costs with no evidence of increased efficacy or reduced risk.

Proposal (d), the use of a precontrol survey for the black-footed ferret, was commented on by USDA, New Mexico and South Dakota. USDA recommended that the Colorado Division of Wildlife or appropriate States be consulted and their historical records of black-footed ferret presence or absence be considered. USDA stated that they did not support a costly and needless survey when there is no sign or record of the species in the area for the last 20 to 30 years. They also recommended that informal consultation or § 7 consultation under the Endangered Species Act involving the appropriate State would suffice rather than the more costly and restrictive modifications of the survey.

New Mexico's comments and recommendations were similar, i.e. reliance on State wildlife agencies and consultation with FWS rather than the survey. South Dakota commented that until procedures for the black-footed ferret survey are formalized, they were unable to comment on their suitability or practicality, however they note that such survey methods should not be so complex and time consuming that they are neither practical or economically feasible.

The Tri-River area Cooperative Extension Service (Colorado) commented that prairie dogs are carriers of disease harmful to humans and must be controlled. They noted that 1080 and strychnine are the most effective means of control.

3. Agency Response

The Agency agrees with commenters that a determination of the most efficacious bait concentration and application rate should be based on field test data. USDA's comment that EPA noted in PD 2/3 that it did not have data to specify a bait concentration of less than 0.11% is correct, but the Agency goes on to explain in PD 2/3 that the Agency was convinced, based on LD50 values that a concentration less than 0.11% would be efficacious and 0.02% appeared to be the best estimate. The Agency notes that the U.S. Forest Service/USDA is conducting 1080 field efficacy studies. These studies should provide an indication of appropriate bait concentration for prairie dog control. The Agency believes that the studies will support the Agency's conclusions that a bait concentration lower than the current .11% will be efficacious.

Based on the concerns raised by commenters about the potential adverse effects from lowering the bait concentration, the Agency has modified its position regarding the use of the .11% bait for the 1985 control season. The details are described in Chapter V.

The Agency response to comments on baiting and post baiting procedures is the same as for ground squirrels. These procedures will be modified accordingly for prairie dog control.

The Agency believes that because of the endangered status and rarity of the black-footed ferret, relying solely on training provided as part of the applicator certification requirements is not sufficient to provide an adequate level of protection. The Agency's intent in PD 2/3 was to allow use by farmers and ranchers under the direct supervision of governmental agency personnel. A decision regarding the distribution and possession of 1080 for prairie dog control will depend on an assessment of the Colorado program for the protection of the black-footed ferret. Clarification of these and other issues, such as training of ranchers and farmers, what constitutes "direct supervision", etc. will be addressed following approval by EPA of a precontrol survey.

A precontrol survey for the black-footed ferret has been the central concern of the Agency in determining whether to allow the continued use of 1080 for prairie dog control. The Agency has asked USDI/FWS, the experts in wildlife management and protection, for an opinion and guidance on the use of a precontrol survey. USDI's position is that a precontrol survey prior to the use of 1080, strychnine and several other toxicants can provide adequate protection for the ferret, provided it is conducted in strict accordance with approved protocols. The Agency, USDI and several state and farm organizations have been seeking to develop and agree upon an adequate survey in connection with the use of strychnine for prairie dog control. However, at this time, there are many elements regarding the precontrol survey that have not been adequately clarified or agreed upon.

The Agency notes in response to USDA's suggestion that historical records of ferret presence or absence and consultation with State wildlife agencies be relied upon to decide if 1080 treatment should proceed might well result in secondary ferret exposure. The black-footed ferret currently has an unknown range, and is very rarely spotted even in areas it is believed to inhabit. In fact, the one known viable population of black-footed ferrets, the group in the Meteetsee mountains of Wyoming was discovered outside what was then considered the range of the species. This argues for the continued use of a precontrol survey in areas of potential black-footed ferret habitat.

The potential human health hazard from diseases carried by the prairie dog was not addressed by EPA. No data or information supporting this contention was submitted by any commenter or from health officials in Colorado or other states.

C. Rangeland, Cropland and Non-Agricultural Sites Except Around Ships and Buildings: Other Rodents

1. Proposed Actions in PD 2/3

In the PD 2/3, the Agency proposed the denial of applications for the control of the following rodents on rangeland: chipmunks, cotton rats, deer mice, kangaroo rats, and meadow mice. The Agency also proposed the denial of applications for the control of Norway rats, cotton rats, and wood rats on croplands as well as denial of applications for chipmunks, cotton rats, Norway rats, kangaroo rats, wood rats, deer mice, and meadow mice on non-agricultural sites.

The Agency proposed denial of these uses because it determined that the uses potentially put nontarget animals at risk and safer alternatives were available. The Agency also noted that because of low usage and the availability of efficacious, economically viable alternatives, the impact on overall benefits was expected to be low.

The Agency proposed to modify the terms and conditions of use for meadow mice control on cropland because this use accounted for the majority of 1080 used on croplands and denial could result in locally severe impacts on benefits because of the increased cost of alternatives. The Agency also concluded that risk reduction measures were available that would enable benefits to outweigh risks. These measures included:

i. Standardize the bait active ingredient concentration at 0.02% and a dosage of one teaspoon for hand baiting or four to five pounds per acre for aerial baiting.

ii. Standardize baiting and post-baiting procedures for hand and aerial application in accordance with the proposed action under "Rangeland and Cropland Rodents: Ground Squirrels."

iii. Prohibit use in the range of the Aleutian Canada goose in accordance with the proposed action under "Rangeland and Cropland Rodents: Ground Squirrels."

The Agency proposed no action for the use of 1080 to control pocket gophers below ground on rangeland, cropland or nonagricultural sites because the Agency believed a potential for substantial risk to nontarget animals was unlikely.

2. Comments on PD 2/3

USDA noted that the PD 2/3 pointed out that no risk to nontarget animals had been substantiated and only minimal amounts of 1080 were used to control the rodents whose product applications were to be denied. They noted that only a single incident had been reported from any of these uses; one involving geese mortality where both 1080 and zinc phosphide were used for control of meadow voles. USDA noted that 1080 was principally used to control highly irruptive populations of rodents that have proven difficult to control with alternative rodenticides and recommended that the uses be maintained. USDA stated that they did not see how the potential risks at these use sites was any greater than for use in and around ships and buildings. USDA also cited the Agency's Preliminary Benefit Analysis conclusion that 1080 is the most efficacious and cost effective single dose rodenticide available for control of field and commensal rodents.

CDFA commented that the risks to nontargets from these uses were minimal and the uses should be retained. New Mexico also stated that cancelling these uses was not justified. Another commenter, Nevada, stated that this proposal should be reconsidered for meadow mice and kangaroo rats, since the alternative pesticides, zinc phosphide and strychnine, were more hazardous to birds than 1080.

3. Agency Response

The Agency maintains that these uses pose some risk to nontarget species, that they have very low benefits, and alternative pesticides are available. However, the Agency is concerned about the the control of irruptive populations of rodents and the possibility of increased risk to avian species from alternative chemicals. Therefore, the Agency will allow the continued use of 1080 to control all of the rodent species proposed for denial in PD 2/3 provided registrants agree to generate the data necessary for Federal registration, and make certain use modifications and labeling changes described in Chapter V.

Although no comments were received on the meadow mouse use on cropland, the Agency will permit the continued use of 1080 for this use at current bait concentration and application rates provided registrants make certain changes in baiting and post baiting procedures and agree to generate the data necessary for Federal registration.

Although no action was proposed for the pocket gopher use and no comments were received, the Agency will call in intrastate products bearing this use for Federal registration. Registrants will be able to continue to use 1080 for this use provided they agree to generate the data necessary for Federal registration.

D. Use In and Around Ships and Buildings: Norway Rat, Roof Rat and House Mice

The Agency proposed no action for the use of 1080 in and around ships and buildings to control these three rodent species. No comments were submitted on the proposal. Although these uses are contained on a Federally registered product, the Agency will require data for these uses.

E. General Comments on Proposed Actions

As a general comment, USDA suggested that no final decision to further restrict or limit the use of 1080 be rendered unless significant risks are demonstrated. While noting the need to monitor and restrict the use of materials and techniques

which present a real and significant threat to humans, domestic
animals, and non-target wildlife species, USDA commented that
we cannot afford to eliminate or regulate to an ineffective status,
needed, efficacious, cost effective control tools based on
assumptions, presumptions, conjecture or noncomparative analogies
and a lack of sufficient field data as presented in PD 2/3.

Several Agencies, most notably CDFA and USDA, have
emphasized the economic importance of 1080 and the significant
adverse effects on the agricultural economy that would result
if 1080 was denied or restricted in the manner proposed in PD
2/3.

In its response to comments, the Agency has noted throughout
this document its support of scientific decisions on the basis
of field data rather than extrapolations from LD50 data.
However, the kinds of data referred to by USDA and other
commenters do not exist. The Agency also notes that the stated
economic importance of 1080 should result in the interested
parties generating data to support the continued use of 1080.

V. Final Regulatory Decision

A. General

There is only one 1080 product that is registered under § 3 of FIFRA. This product, which is a technical grade material, bears directions for use to control certain rodents in and around buildings and ships. Its label, however, does not contain any use directions for control of field rodents. All 1080 products that bear use directions for field rodent control are intrastate products, except for a "special local needs" registration in Oregon.

Intrastate products are distributed in only three states, California, Colorado and Nevada. In other states where 1080 was used at one time for field rodent control, users relied on the U.S. Department of the Interior's 1080 product. The registration of this product was withdrawn following an Executive Order prohibiting the use of 1080 on Federal lands.

In order for EPA to implement the regulatory position of this document, intrastate products must be "called in" for Federal registration. Intrastate producers who wish to continue to sell and distribute their products must submit an application for Federal registration. In addition, intrastate producers must agree to: 1) provide the data necessary for Federal registration, 2) modify procedures and product labeling as described in this chapter, and 3) adhere to the schedule found in Appendix A for submittal of data. The Agency will consider the submittal of the application for Federal registration as demonstrating the intent to provide the necessary data. Failure to submit an application in a timely manner or to adhere to the other requirements of continued use may result in the denial of the application for Federal registration and a prohibition against the sale, distribution and use of the 1080 product in question.

Oregon's § 24(c) registrant and the registrant of technical 1080 will be required to provide a full complement of data to support their registrations. A data call in under FIFRA § 3(c)(2)(B) will be issued to these registrants. Failure to respond in a timely manner or commit to the generation of data may result in the Agency suspending these registrations.

The Oregon § 24(c) registrant will have to modify his product label in accordance with this document. The technical registrant will also be requred to make certain label changes. Specific changes will be detailed in notices sent to each registrant.

The Agency will continue to allow the use of 1080 to control all field rodent species identified on current intrastate and Federal products at current bait concentrations, except for the control of ground squirrels in the range of the California condor and for the control of prairie dogs in Colorado. These uses will be permitted at current bait concentrations during 1985. Beginning in 1986, however, bait concentrations for prairie dog control must be reduced to .02% unless efficacy data are generated. If efficacy data show that .02% is not effective, the Agency will consider changes in the bait concentration provided data are available that establish the lowest effective concentration level and the Agency can determine that use at that level will not impact the black-footed ferret.

If 1080 use is permitted in the range of the condor, after 1985, such use will be at a maximum bait concentration of .02% unless field efficiacy data are submitted demonstrating that the .02% level is not effective as well as data establishing the lowest effective bait concentration. The Agency must also determine if higher bait concentration will impact the condor. A decision on the use of 1080 in the range of the condor has been delayed pending discussions with the Office of Endangered Species (OES).

The Agency recently received a biological opinion from the Office of Endangered Species (OES) stating that use of the 1080 livestock protection collar in the range of the California condor would jeopardize the continued existence of this species. The OES opinion emphasized that there are only a few condors in existence and there is uncertainty about the effects of the collar on the condor. Although there are substantial differences in potential 1080 exposure from the livestock protection collar and treated grain bait, the drastic decline in the condor population (OES reported one source estimated 9 to 11 condors in the wild) may require prohibition of 1080 use in the range of the condor until safety data are evaluated by the Agency. A decision on the use of 1080 in the range of the condor will be made following discussion with OES. The decision will be made by January 1, 1986.

Compound 1080 has been classified as a restricted use pesticide, i.e. it can only be used by a certified applicator or someone under the direct supervision of a certified applicator. Restricted use classification does not apply to intrastate products although generally states have limited the sale and use of intrastate products to certified applicators if EPA has restricted a corresponding Federal product or active ingredient. As a condition of continued use, intrastate products will now be required to bear the restricted use label statements contained in 40 CFR 162.10(j)(2). The addition of the restricted use labeling on intrastate products does not negate the necessity of maintaining current limitations on supervision, use, possession, storage and disposal of 1080 required on current labels.

The Agency has concluded that all 1080 grain baits must be dyed a unique standardized color. Available information indicates that Auramine O, a yellow dye used in California, does not appear to impact on avian species. This may be the result of repellency caused by the dye. Therefore, until data are submitted supporting the use of another dye color, the Agency is requiring that all 1080 grain baits used for field rodent control be dyed yellow. The producer of technical 1080 will be required to add a dye statement to the product label. This statement is contained in section (F)(1)(d) of this chapter.

Other applicants seeking Federal registration of any field rodent use of 1080 must submit the data to obtain a Federal registration prior to using 1080. The Agency believes it is necessary that any expansion of the use of 1080 to other states be predicated on an adequate data base to support such expansion.

Registrants and intrastate producers will have 30 days to submit an application for amended registration or regis-tration respectively, following receipt of notification from EPA. Each registrant or intrastate producer will be notified of the requirements for compliance with this document by certified mail. All 1080 intrastate products and the 24(c) product that are sold, used, distributed, or released for shipment after December 31, 1985, must comply with the applicable parts of this chapter. Any 1080 product used for reformulation that is released for shipment after December 31, 1985, must comply with the applicable parts of this section. Existing stocks, except where specified otherwise, may be used with a modified label after December 31, 1985.

As the data for Federal registration are submitted and reviewed by the Agency, additional modifications in the terms and conditions of use of 1080 products may be required. After reviewing the data, the Agency may also determine that some or all uses of a particular product should not be permitted and will cancel the registration or deny the application for Federal registration, which ever is appropriate, for those uses in question.

The following sections in this chapter describe the requirements necessary for the continued use of existing 1080 products. Section F of this chapter details all of the requirements.

B. Rangeland, Cropland and Non-Agricultural Sites:
   Ground Squirrels

   1. Reduction and Standardization of Bait Concentration
      and Application Rates

   The Agency has decided to allow use at current label
bait concentrations until efficacy data are generated,
except in the range of the California condor.

   The Agency is concerned that use of ineffective baits
might result in overbaiting, increase costs to producers,
and might lead to the development of more 1080 resistant
populations of ground squirrel. Because of these concerns,
the Agency believes, where appropriate, it is prudent to
base bait concentration levels on efficacy data. However,
the precarious nature of the condor population requires, at
a minimum, imposition of lower bait concentrations. It is
possible for reasons discussed earlier in this chapter that
the Agency may prohibit the use of 1080 in the range of the
condor until data are submitted showing that the use of 1080
will not jeopardize the continued existence of the species.

   Because of the timing of the release of the PD 4, reduction
of bait concentrations for 1985 baiting programs cannot be
implemented. However, beginning in 1986 if 1080 use in the
range of the condor is permitted, baits must be at a maximum
concentration of .02% unless field efficacy data are submitted
demonstrating that the .02% level is not effective as well as
data establishing the lowest effective bait concentration.
The Agency must also determine if higher bait concentrations
will impact the California condor. A label statement regarding
use of 1080 at the .02% level will be required if use in the
range of the condor is permitted. This statement is presented
in section F of this chapter.

   The Agency believes that its calculation of an efficacious
bait concentration level of .02%, which was based on available
LD 50 data and is consistent with Spencer's laboratory
observations (1946), will be substantiated by field efficacy
testing.

   The generation of efficacy data establishing the lowest
efficacious bait concentration will be one of the first
requirements of applicants in support of Federal registration
of their product.

   2. Standardization of Hand Baiting and Post-Baiting
      Procedures

   Concerning the standardization of hand baiting and
post-baiting procedures, the Agency concludes that the requirement

to keep pets and domestic animals away is overly restrictive, and would, as a practical matter, prohibit use since there are very few places where free-roaming pets and livestock do not occasionally occur. Therefore the label statement has been revised to read:

> Do not expose baits in manner which presents a likely hazard to pets, poultry, or livestock.

The Agency has concluded that the proposed requirement to bury or burn all visible carcasses cannot be reasonably implemented in some situations and has revised this requirement. Therefore the label statement has been revised to read:

> Where possible, pick up and burn or bury deeply all visible carcasses of animals killed by 1080.

3. Standardization of Aerial Baiting and Post-Baiting Procedures

The Agency has revised the proposed procedures for disposal of carcasses to be consistent with those for hand baiting procedures. Specific requirements for aerial baiting are presented in section (F)(2)(b) of this chapter.

4. Special Restrictions for Endangered Species Protection

As noted in Chapter IV, the Agency has withdrawn the seasonal and geographic restrictions proposed for continued use of 1080 in California. Compound 1080 bait products used in California will be required to bear the following endangered species statement:

> Notice: The killing of a member of an endangered species during compound 1080 baiting operations may result in a fine and/or imprisonment under the Endangered Species Act. Before baiting, the user is advised to contact the the local Fish and Game Office for specific information on endangered species. Do not use compound 1080 in the geographic ranges of the following species except under programs and procedures approved by the USEPA: California condor, San Joaquin kit fox, Aleutian Canada goose, Morro Bay kangaroo rat, and salt marsh harvest mouse. Users must contact the local fish and Game Office for specific information on EPA approved programs and procedures regarding endangered species.

Other states, as appropriate, will be required to incorporate a statement similar to the one above on products used to control ground squirrels. This statement is contained in section (F)(2)(c) of this chapter.

In PD 2/3 the Agency's proposed actions concerning the black-footed ferret were limited to risks associated with the control of prairie dogs. However, the black-footed ferret is also potentially at risk from ground squirrel control operations. The Agency is requiring that the following use restriction be placed on the Colorado 1080 product label for prairie dog control:

> Do not use for ground squirrel control within 200 yards of prairie dog colonies unless a precontrol survey for the black-footed ferret has been performed prior to control and produces no evidence that a black-footed ferret is present in the survey area. Do not use within five miles of a prairie dog colony where a black-footed ferret has been confirmed to be present.

5. Other Label Statements

Additional label statements concerning hazard to nontarget wildlife, restricted use classification, and bait dyes are contained in section F of this chapter.

C. Rangeland and Cropland: Prairie Dogs

The Agency has concluded that the bait concentration for prairie dog control should be lowered to .02% in the absence of any data that demonstrates this level does not provide an effective level of control. As a practical matter, the timing of the release of this document precludes Colorado from reducing bait concentrations for the 1985 season. However, beginning in 1986 the use of 1080 for prairie dog control will be at a maximum bait concentration of .02% unless field efficacy data are submitted demonstrating that the .02% level is not effective as well as data establishing the lowest effective bait concentration. The Agency must also determine if higher bait concentrations will impact the endangered black-footed ferret. A label statement regarding use of 1080 at the .02% level for prairie dog control is required and is presented in section (F)(3)(a) of this chapter.

The Agency has made changes in the proposed baiting and post-baiting procedures consistent with those procedures for ground squirrels. These procedures are detailed in Section F of this chapter. Other label statements concerning endangered species, hazard to nontarget wildlife, restricted use classification, and bait dyes are contained in section F of this chapter.

The Agency has concluded that the use of 1080 for prairie dog control in Colorado should be by government agency personnel or under the direct supervision of such personnel. As with the reduction in bait concentration, the Agency will not require changes in the 1985 Colorado program. Specific details regarding use supervision, possession and storage of 1080, etc. will be resolved if a precontrol survey is approved for the black-footed ferret.

Use after December 31, 1985, will require the use of an EPA approved program including a precontrol survey for the black-footed ferret. Colorado should submit the precontrol survey by January 1986, in order to allow the Agency adequate review time.

Other states seeking to use 1080 for prairie dog control must obtain a § 3 registration prior to use.

D. Rangeland, Cropland and Non-Agricultural Sites Except Around Ships and Buildings: Other Rodents

The Agency has concluded that the uses proposed for denial in PD 2/3 can be continued provided registrants agree to generate the data necessary for Federal registration, submit this data on schedule, and make certain modifications in baiting and post-baiting procedures, add endangered species precautions and restricted use label statements and comply with the requirements of this document. These same conditions apply to meadow mice on cropland, which was proposed for continued use in PD 2/3. The same limitations on use in the range of the condor as required for ground squirrels apply to these rodent species. The uses proposed for denial in PD 2/3 were:

    (1) Rangeland: chipmunks, cotton rats, deer mice, kangaroo rats and meadow mice.

    (2) Cropland: Norway rats,cotton rats and wood rats.

    (3) Non-Agricultural Sites: chipmunks, cotton rats, Norway rats, kangaroo rats, wood rats, deer mice and meadow mice.

The specific requirements of continued use are detailed in section F of this chapter.

No action was proposed in PD 2/3 for pocket gophers. Registrants of this use will be "called in" and will have to agree to generate data for Federal registration.

E. Use In and Around Ships and Buildings: Norway Rat, Roof Rat and House Mice

Although these uses are contained on a Federally registered product, the Agency will require the full complement of data necessary for registration under § 3 of FIFRA.

F. Regulatory Requirements

1. General Requirements

All intrastate products will be "called in" for Federal registration. A § 3(c)(2)(B) data call in notice will be issued for the § 24(c) product in Oregon and for the technical 1080 product. The § 24(c) registrant and the technical registrant will be required to submit a full complement of data identified in Appendix A to support the continued registration of their products.

All applicants for Federal registration and current Federal registrants will be allowed to continue selling, distributing and using their products provided they:

° Commit to generate the data necessary for Federal registration under § 3 of FIFRA and submit the data on schedule as outlined in Appendix A.

° Make certain changes in baiting and post-baiting procedures, add endangered species and nontarget precautions and restricted use statements to product labels and comply with the other requirements specified in this chapter.

The following requirements apply to all field rodent use products containing 1080:

a. Hand Baiting and Post-Baiting Procedures

The following procedures are to be placed on all 1080 product labels:

   i. Baiting should not be done unless tests indicate satisfactory bait acceptance will occur in areas to be treated.
  ii. Do not expose baits in a manner which presents a likely hazard to pets, poultry, or livestock.
 iii. Clean up all accidentally spilled bait immediately.
  iv. Do not place bait in piles.
   v. Where possible, pick up and burn or bury deeply all visible carcasses of animals killed by 1080.
  vi. Do not use within 1/4 mile of a dwelling without first notifying the occupants.

b. Nontarget Species Label Precaution

The following statement must be placed on all 1080 product labels:

This product is very highly toxic to wildlife.
Birds and mammals feeding on target organisms
or treated bait may be killed. Keep out of any
body of water. Apply this product only as
specified on this label.

c. Restricted Use Classification Label Statement

All 1080 products may be used only by certified applicators
or persons under their direct supervision in addition to any current
use supervision requirements or restrictions. All 1080 products
must bear the restricted use label statements specified in
40 CFR 162.10(j)(2). The statement "Restricted Use Pesticide"
must appear on the front panel of the label. Directly below
"Restricted Use Pesticide" the following statement is required:

For retail sale to and use only by Certified Applicators
or persons under their direct supervision and only
for those uses covered by the Certified Applicator's
certification.

Modifications in this statement will be permitted to reflect
state requirements limiting sale, distribution and possesion of
1080.

d. Bait Dyes

Any bait containing directions for use to control field
rodents must be dyed yellow. The label of any 1080 product
that contains directions for formulating end-use baits for
field rodent control must contain the following statement:

Formulators must ensure that all compound 1080 grain
baits used for field rodent control are dyed yellow.

The label of any 1080 product that contains directions
for formulating end-use baits for commensal rodent control
must contain the following statement:

Compound 1080 grain baits used for commensal rodent
control must be dyed in accordance with USDA
regulations.

2. Rangeland, Cropland and Non-Agricultural Sites: Ground Squirrels

In addition to the requirements cited in section 1 of
this chapter, 1080 products bearing directions for use for
the control of ground squirrels must comply with the
following requirements.

a. Bait Concentration Levels

All products may continue to be used at current bait concentration levels until efficacy data are generated to establish the lowest efficacious concentrations, except in the range of the California condor. Through December 31, 1985, use of 1080 in the range of the condor may continue under present label conditions. However, as noted in section A of this chapter, a recent jeopardy opinion from OES on the livestock protection collar necessitates further evaluation of the use of 1080 grain baits in the range of the condor. Beginning in 1986, if permitted, the use of 1080 in the range of the condor will be at a maximum bait concentration of .02% unless field efficacy data are submitted demonstrating that the .02% level is not effective as well as data establishing the lowest effective bait concentration. The Agency must also determine if higher bait concentrations will impact the California condor.

The following statement must be placed on 1080 product labels used for ground squirrel control in California if use in the range of the condor is permitted:

> Baits at concentrations greater than .02% may not be used in the range of the California condor.

b. Aerial Baiting and Post-Baiting Procedures

The following statement must be placed on 1080 product labels used for ground squirrel control in California:

i. Use in accordance with the Guidelines for Applying Rodent Baits by Aircraft for Control of Ground Squirrels in the California Vertebrate Pest Control Handbook.
ii. Where possible, pick up and burn or bury deeply all visible carcasses of animals killed by 1080.

Aerial application of 1080 baits may continue in other states as permitted by current labels. However, applicants for Federal registration must submit aerial application procedures and guidelines for Agency review at the time they submit the application for Federal registration. A reference to these procedures will be incorporated on the appropriate product label.

c. Endangered Species Label Precautions

The following statement must be placed on 1080 product labels used for ground squirrel control in California:

Notice: The killing of a member of an endangered species during compound 1080 baiting operations may result in a fine and/or imprisonment under the Endangered Species Act. Before baiting, the user must contact the local Fish and Game Office for specific information on endangered species. Do not use compound 1080 baits in the geographic ranges of the following species except under programs and procedures approved by the USEPA: California condor, San Joaquin kit fox, Aleutian Canada goose, Morro Bay kangaroo rat, and salt marsh harvest mouse.

The following statement must be placed on 1080 product labels used for ground squirrel control in Colorado, Nevada and Oregon.

Notice: The killing of a member of an endangered species during compound 1080 baiting operations may result in a fine and/or imprisonment under the Endangered Species Act. Before baiting, the user must contact the local Fish and Game Office or the Regional Office of the Fish and Wildlife Service for specific information on endangered species.

The following statement must be placed on 1080 product labels used for ground squirrel control in and around prairie dog colonies:

Do not use for ground squirrel control within 200 yards of prairie dog colonies unless a precontrol survey for the black-footed ferret has been performed prior to control and the use of such survey produces no evidence that a black-footed ferret is present in the survey area. Do not use within five miles of a prairie dog colony where the presence of a black-footed ferret has been confirmed to be present.

3. Rangeland and Cropland: Prairie Dogs

In addition to the requirements cited in section 1 of this chapter, the 1080 product bearing directions for use for the control of prairie dogs must comply with the following requirements:

a. Bait Concentration Levels

This product may continue to be used at current bait concentration levels and label conditions through December 31, 1985. Beginning in 1986, the use of 1080 for prairie dog control will be at a maximum bait concentration of .02% unless field efficacy data are submitted demonstrating that the .02% level is not effective as well as data establishing

the lowest effective bait concentration. The Agency must
also determine if higher bait concentrations will impact the
endangered black-footed ferret.

The following statement must be placed on any 1080 product
used to control prairie dogs:

Baits at concentrations greater than .02% may
not be used for the control of prairie dogs.

b. Use Supervision

The following statement must be placed on any 1080 product
used to control prairie dogs:

The use of 1080 for prairie dog control is restricted to
governmental agencies or persons under the direct
supervision of members of governmental agencies.

c. Precontrol Survey for the Black-footed Ferret

The following statement must be placed on any 1080 product
used to control prairie dogs:

Compound 1080 can be used for the control of prairie
dogs only if an EPA-approved survey for the black-footed
ferret has been performed prior to control and the use
of such a survey produces no evidence that a black-footed
ferret is present in the survey area.

d. Endangered Species Label Precautions

The following statement must be placed on any 1080 product
used to control prairie dogs:

Notice: The killing of a member of an endangered species
during compound 1080 baiting operations may result in a
fine and/or imprisonment under the Endangered Species
Act. Before baiting, the user must contact the local
Fish and Game Office or the Regional Office of the Fish
and Wildlife Service for specific information on endangered
species.

4. Rangeland, Cropland and Non-Agricultural Sites Except Around Ships and Buildings: Other Rodents

° Rangeland: chipmunks, cotton rats, deer mice,
  kangaroo rats and meadow mice.

° Cropland: meadow mice, Norway rats, cotton rats and
  wood rats.

° Non-Agricultural Sites: chipmunks, cotton rats, Norway rats, kangaroo rats, wood rats, deer mice and meadow mice.

In addition to the requirements cited in section 1 of this chapter, 1080 products bearing directions for use for the control of the above rodents must comply with the following requirements:

a. Bait Concentration Levels

All products may continue to be used at current bait concentration levels until efficacy data are generated to establish the lowest efficacious concentrations, except in the range of the California condor. Through December 31, 1985, use of 1080 in the range of the condor may continue under present label conditions. However, beginning in 1986 the use of 1080 in the range of the condor will be at a maximum bait concentration of .02% unless field efficacy data are submitted demonstrating that the .02% level is not effective, that another higher level is effective, and that the higher bait concentration will not adversely affect the condor.

The following statement must be placed on 1080 product labels used for rodent control in California:

Baits at concentrations greater than .02% may not be used in the range of the California condor.

b. Endangered Species Label Precautions

The following statement is to be placed on all 1080 products used in California for control of rodents identified in section (F)(4):

Notice: The killing of a member of an endangered species during compound 1080 baiting operations may result in a fine and/or imprisonment under the Endangered Species Act. Before baiting, the user must contact the local Fish and Game Office for specific information on endangered species. Do not use compound 1080 baits in the geographic ranges of the following species except under programs and procedures approved by the USEPA: California condor, San Joaquin kit fox, Aleutian Canada goose, Morro Bay kangaroo rat, and salt marsh harvest mouse.

The following statement is to be placed on all 1080 products used in states other than California for control of rodents identified in section (F)(4):

Notice: The killing of a member of an endangered species during compound 1080 baiting operations may result in a fine and/or imprisonment under the Endangered Species Act. Before baiting, the user must contact the local Fish and Game Office or the Regional Office of the Fish and Wildlife Service for specific information on endangered species.

5. Pocket Gophers

No additional label modifications are required for this use at this time except the restricted use statement contained in section (F)(1)(c) and the bait dye statement contained in (F)(1)(d) of this chapter.

6. Use In and Around Ships and Buildings: Norway Rat, Roof

Rat and House Mice

No additional label modifications are required for this use at this time except the dye color statement contained in section (F)(1)(d) of this chapter.

VI. BIBLIOGRAPHY

Fish and Wildlife Service correspondence. July 21, 1978.

Hagen, H., 1972. A review of the use of toxic chemicals for mammalian animal control in California. California Department of Fish and Game, Wildlife Management Administration Report No. 72-75.

Hegdal, P.L., Gatz, T.A., Fite, E.C., 1980. Secondary effects of rodenticides on mammalian predators. Denver Wildlife Research Center. (Unpublished).

Hegdal, P.L., Gatz, T.A., Fagerstone, K.A., Glahn, J.F., Matsche, G.H., 1979. Hazards to wildlife associated with 1080 baiting for California ground squirrels. Final report of the U.S. Fish and Wildlife Service under Interagency Agreement EPA-IGA-D7-0449.

Ketron, Inc., 1979. Assessment of the environmental effects of predator and rodent control programs in Wyoming using strychnine and 1080. KFR 232-79.

Marsh, R.E., 1967. Aircraft as a means of baiting ground squirrels. Proc. 3rd Vert Control Conf., San Francisco, March 7-9, 1967. pp 2-6.

Myers, K., 1980. Zoology Department, University of Guelph, Ontario. Personal communication.

Pearson, O.P., 1966. The prey of carnivores during one cycle of mouse abundance. J. Animal Ecology., 35:217-233.

Pearson, O.P., 1971. Additional measurements of the impact of carnivores on California voles. (Microtus californicus). J. Mammal., 52:41-49.

Schitoskey, F., 1975. Primary and secondary hazards of three rodenticides to kit fox. J. Wildl. Mgmt., 39(2):416-418.

Sibley,F.C., 1966. 1080 squirrel poisoning operation. Bureau of Sport Fish and Wildlife.

Spencer, D.A., 1946. Compound 1080 - Sodium Flouroacetate, As a control agent for field rodents. National Research Council Insect Control Committee Report No. 161. Partial interim report.

Swick, C.D., 1973. Determination of San Joaquin kit fox range in Contra Costa, Alameda, San Joaquin, and Tulare Counties. State of California Department of Fish and Game.

Swick, C.D., 1973. San Joaquin kit fox - an impact report of secondary hazards of aerial application of 1080 grain baits for ground squirrel control in San Luis Obispo County. State of California Department of Fish and Game.

Tucker, R.K., 1965-1972. Internal report series in pharmacology. United States Department of the Interior, Fish and Wildlife Service, Denver Wildlife Research Center (Unpublished).

United States Environmental Protection Agency. Position Document 1. Rebuttable Presumption Against Registration: Compound 1080.

United States Environmental Protection Agency. Position Document 2/3. Sodium Monoflouroacetate (Compound 1080).

United States Environmental Protection Agency, Science Advisory Panel. Report of the Ad Hoc Study Group on Sodium Monoflouroacetate. Washington D.C. July 3, 1984.

Wagner, F.H. and L.C. Stoddart, 1972. Influence of coyote predation on black-tailed jackrabbit population in Utah. Journal of Wildlife Management., 36(2):329-342.

APPENDIX A

DATA REQUIREMENTS* AND SUBMISSION SCHEDULE

FOR COMPOUND 1080 REGISTRATION

158.120 PRODUCT CHEMISTRY DATA REQUIREMENTS:

Product Identity:	Guideline Reference	Time Allowed To Submit Study Results to EPA
Identity of Ingredients	61-1	6 months
Statement of Composition	61-2	1 year
Discussion of Formation of Ingredients	61-3	1 year

Analysis & Certification of Product Ingredients:		
Certification of Limits	62-2	6 months
Analytical Method for Enforcement of limits	62-3	1 year

Physical & Chemical Properties:		
Color	63-2	1 year
Physical State	63-3	1 year
Odor	63-4	1 year
Melting Point	63-5	1 year
Boiling Point	63-6	1 year
Density, Bulk Density, or Specific Gravity	63-7	1 year
Solubility	63-8	1 year
Vapor Pressure	63-9	1 year
Dissociation Constant	63-10	1 year
Octanol/Water Partition Coefficient	63-11	1 year
pH	63-12	1 year
Stability	63-13	1 year
Oxidizing or Reducing Action	63-14	1 year
Flammability	63-15	1 year
Explodability	63-16	1 year
Storage Stability	63-17	1 year
Viscosity	63-18	1 year
Miscibility	63-19	1 year
Corrosion Characteristics	63-20	1 year
Dielectric Breakdown Voltage	63-21	1 year

*Agency review of these data may require the development of additional safety data or benefits data. The specific data requirements that apply to basic producers and end users will be identified in the Notice "Calling In" intrastate products for registration and in the 3(c)(2)(B) data call in notice sent to Federal registrants. If the basic producer does not agree to generate the required data, end users must agree to submit such data. Some of the data requirements of this Appendix may already have been satisfied in conjunction with the registration of the livestock protection collar or other registration activities.

158.125 RESIDUE CHEMISTRY DATA REQUIREMENTS:

Registrants must submit a detailed description of each use with their application for Federal registration.
This information will be used by the Agency to determine if a particular use is a food or non-food use. The information needed for each use site includes:

(1) How the bait is applied, e.g. bait box, broadcast ground application, aerial application.

(2) Rate of application.

(3) The number or frequency of applications.

(4) The minimum interval between applications.

If EPA determines what a particular use is a food use, applicants will be notified of which data requirements listed below will be applicable.

		Time Allowed to Submit Study Results to EPA*
Chemical Identity	171-2	1 year
Directions for Use	171-3	1 year

Nature of Residue:

Plants	171-4	3 years
Livestock	171-4	2 years

Residue Analytical Method and
Magnitude of the Residue:

Crop Field Trials	171-4	2 years
Processed Food/Feed	171-4	2 years
Meat/Milk/Poultry/Eggs	171-4	2 years
Potable Water	171-4	2 years

Reduction of Residue	171-5	2 years
Proposed Tolerance (includes $40,000 filing fee)	171-6	2 years
Reasonable Grounds in Support of Petition	171-7	2 years
Submittal of Analytical Reference Standards	171-13	

* Time begins following determination of food use.

158.130 ENVIRONMENTAL FATE DATA REQUIREMENTS:

Time Allowed
to Submit Study
Results to EPA

Degradation Studies (Lab):

Hydrolysis	161-1	1 year
Photodegradation: On Soil	161-3	1 year

Metabolism Studies (Lab):

Aerobic Soil	161-1	3 years
Anaerobic Aquatic	162-3	3 years

Mobility Studies:

Leaching (Absorption/Desorption	163-1	1 year

158.135 TOXICOLOGY DATA REQUIREMENTS:

Acute Testing:

Dermal LD50 - Rabbit (Preferred Species)	81-2	1 year
Primary Eye Irritation - Rabbit	81-4	1 year
Primary Dermal Irritation - Rabbit	81-5	1 year
Dermal Sensitization - Guinea Pig	81-6	1 year

The following tests will be necessary if 1080 tolerances are required.

Subchronic Testing:

90-Day Feeding:

Rodent	82-1	9 months
Non-Rodent (Dog)	82-1	15 months
21-Day Dermal - Rabbit	82-2	6 months
90-Day Dermal	82-3	9 months
90-Day Inhalation	82-4	9 months
90-Day Neurotoxicity - Hen, Mammal	82-5	9 months

Chronic Testing:

Chronic Feeding:

2 spp. Rodent & Non-Rodent (Dog)	83-1	4 years
Oncogenicity Study:		
2 spp. Rat & Mouse (Preferred)	83-2	4 years
Teratogenicity (2 Species) - Rat mouse, hamster, Rabbit	83-3	9 months
Reproduction (2-Generation) Rat or other species	83-4	2 1/2 years

Mutagenicity Testing:

Gene Mutation (Ames Test)	84-2	6 months
Chromosomal Aberration	84-2	6 months
Other Mechanisms of Mutagenicity	84-4	6 months

Special Testing:

General Metabolism - Rat	85-1	1 year
Dermal Penetration	85-2	6 months
Special Requirement:		
Domestic Animal Safety	86-1	*

* Variable depending on species and type of study basis

158.145 WILDLIFE AND AQUATIC ORGANISM DATA REQUIREMENTS:

Time Allowed
to Submit Study
Register to EPA

Avian and Mammalian Testing:

		Time Allowed to Submit Study Register to EPA
Field efficacy data to establish the lowest effective bait concentration.		1 year
Ferret Mortality Study		1 year
Ferret Survey Study		1 year
Protocol for Ferret Survey Study		4 months
Avian Oral LD50	71-1	1 year
Avian Dietary LC50	71-2	1 year
Avian Reproduction	71-4	3 years
Avian and Mammalian Secondary Hazard Studies		1 year
*Simulated & Actual Field Testing- mammals and birds	71-5	1.5 - 3 years depends upon number of years to be examined

Aquatic Organism Testing:

Freshwater Fish LC50	72-1	1 year
Acute LC50 Freshwater Invertebrates	72-2	1 year
*Fish Early Life Stage and Aquatic Invertebrate Lifecycle		1 year
*Fish - Lifecycle	72-5	1.5 year
*Aquatic Organism Accumulation	72-6	9 months
*Simulated or Actual Field Testing - Aquatic Organisms	72-7	1.5 - 3 years depends upon number of years

* Reserved - depends on results of above tests.

9 781249 502104